# An Autobiography of Buffalo Bill

# An Autobiography of Buffalo Bill

By

William Frederick

# An Autobiography of Buffalo Bill

*by*

William Frederick



Published by

Delhi Open Books

G/F, 4771/23, Bharat Ram Road, Daryaganj,
New Delhi-110002
Ph.: 91-11-42408081
E-mail: delhiopenbooks2016@gmail.com

ISBN: 978-93-90997-66-4

Cover, Typesetting, and Book Design by **Tarun, Rohit**

# Contents



❒

# Chapter-1.

I am about to take the back-trail through the Old West—the West that I knew and loved. All my life it has been a pleasure to show its beauties, its marvels and its possibilities to those who, under my guidance, saw it for the first time.

Now, going back over the ground, looking at it through the eyes of memory, it will be a still greater pleasure to take with me the many readers of this book. And if, in following me through some of the exciting scenes of the old days, meeting some of the brave men who made its stirring history, and listening to my camp-fire tales of the buffalo, the Indian, the stage-coach and the pony-express, their interest in this vast land of my youth, should be awakened, I should feel richly repaid.

The Indian, tamed, educated and inspired with a taste for white collars and moving-pictures, is as numerous as ever, but not so picturesque. On the little tracts of his great inheritance allotted him by civilization he is working out his own manifest destiny.

The buffalo has gone. Gone also is the stagecoach whose progress his pilgrimages often used to interrupt. Gone is the pony express, whose marvelous efficiency could compete with the wind, but not with the harnessed lightning flashed over the telegraph wires. Gone are the very bone-gatherers who laboriously collected the bleaching relics of the great herds that once dotted the prairies.

But the West of the old times, with its strong characters, its stern battles and its tremendous stretches of loneliness, can never be blotted from my mind. Nor can it, I hope, be blotted from the memory of the American people, to whom it has now become a priceless possession.

It has been my privilege to spend my working years on the frontier. I have known and served with commanders like Sherman, Sheridan, Miles, Custer and A.A. Carr—men who would be leaders in any army in any age. I have known and helped to fight with many of the most notable of the Indian warriors.

Frontiersmen good and bad, gunmen as well as inspired prophets of the future, have been my camp companions. Thus, I know the country of which I am about to write as few men now living have known it.

Recently, in the hope of giving permanent form to the history of the Plains, I staged many of the Indian battles for the films. Through the courtesy of the War and Interior Departments I had the help of the soldiers and the Indians.

Now that this work has been done I am again in the saddle and at your service for what I trust will be a pleasant and perhaps instructive journey over the old trails. We shall omit the hazards and the hardships, but often we shall leave the iron roads over which the Pullman rolls and, back in the hills, see the painted Indians winding up the draws, or watch the more savage Mormon Danites swoop down on the wagon-train. In my later years I have brought the West to the East—under a tent. Now I hope to bring the people of the East and of the New West to the Old West, and possibly here and there to supply new material for history.

I shall try to vary the journey, for frequent changes of scenes are grateful to travelers. I shall show you some of the humors as well as the excitements of the frontier. And our last halting-place will be at sunrise—the sunrise of the New West, with its waving grain-fields, fenced flocks and splendid cities, drawing upon the mountains for the water to make it fertile, and upon the whole world for men to make it rich.

I was born on a farm near Leclair, Scott County, Iowa, February 26, 1846. My father, Isaac Cody, had emigrated to what was then a frontier State. He and his people, as well as my mother, had all dwelt in Ohio. I remember that there were Indians all about us, looking savage enough as they slouched about the village streets or loped along the roads on their ponies. But they bore no hostility toward anything save work and soap and water.

We were comfortable and fairly prosperous on the little farm. My mother, whose maiden name was Mary Ann Leacock, took an active part in the life of the neighborhood. An education was scarce in those days. Even school teachers did not always possess it. Mother's education was far beyond the average, and the local school board used to require all applicants for teachers' position to be examined by her before they were entrusted with the tender intellects of the pioneer children.

But the love of adventure was in father's blood. The railroad—the only one I had ever seen—extended as far as Port Byron, Illinois, just across the Mississippi. When the discovery of gold in California in 1849 set the whole country wild, this railroad began to bring the Argonauts, bound for the long overland wagon journey across the Plains. Naturally father caught the excitement. In 1850 he made a start, but it was abandoned—why I never knew. But after that he was not content with Iowa. In 1853 our farm and most of our goods and chattels were converted into money. And in 1854 we all set out for Kansas, which was soon to be opened for settlers as a Territory.

Two wagons carried our household goods. A carriage was provided for my mother and sisters. Father had a trading-wagon built, and stocked it with red blankets, beads, and other goods with which to tempt the Indians. My only brother had been killed by a fall from a horse, so I was second in command, and proud I was of the job.

My uncle Elijah kept a general store at Weston, Missouri, just across the Kansas line. He was a large exporter of hemp as well as a trader. Also he was a slave-owner.

Weston was our first objective. Father had determined to take up a claim in Kansas and to begin a new life in this stirring country. Had he foreseen the dreadful consequences to himself and to his family of this decision we might have remained in Iowa, in which case perhaps I might have grown up an Iowa farmer, though that now seems impossible.

Thirty days of a journey that was a constant delight to me brought us to Weston, where we left the freight-wagons and mother and my sisters in the care of my uncle.

To my great joy father took me with him on his first trip into Kansas—where he was to pick out his claim and incidentally to trade with the Indians from our wagon. I shall never forget the thrill that ran through me when father, pointing to the block-house at Fort Leavenworth, said:

"Son, you now see a real military fort for the first time in your life." And a real fort it was. Cavalry—or dragoons as they called them then—were engaged in saber drill, their swords flashing in the sunlight. Artillery was rumbling over the parade ground. Infantry was marching and wheeling. About the Post were men dressed all in buckskin with coonskin caps or broad-brimmed slouch hats—real Westerners of whom I had dreamed. Indians of all sorts were loafing about—all friendly, but a new and different kind of Indians from any I had seen—Kickapoos, Possawatomies, Delawares, Choctaws, and other tribes, of which I had often heard. Everything I saw fascinated me.

These drills at the Fort were no fancy dress-parades. They meant business. A thousand miles to the west the Mormons were running things in Utah with a high hand. No one at Fort Leavenworth doubted that these very troops would soon be on their way to determine whether Brigham Young or the United States Government should be supreme there.

To the north and west the hostile Indians, constantly irritated by the encroachments of the white man, had become a growing menace. The block-houses I beheld were evidences of preparedness against this danger. And in that day the rumblings of the coming struggle over slavery could already be heard. Kansas—very soon afterward "Bleeding Kansas"—was destined to be an early battleground. And we were soon to know something of its tragedies.

Free-soil men and pro-slavery men were then ready to rush across the border the minute it was opened for settlement. Father was a Free-soil man. His brother Elijah who, as I have said, was a slave-owner, was a believer in the extension of slavery into the new territory.

Knowing that the soldiers I saw today might next week be on their way to battle made my eyes big with excitement. I could have stayed there forever. But father had other plans, and we were soon on our way. With our trading- wagon we climbed a hill—later named Sheridan's Ridge for General Philip Sheridan. From its summit we had a view of Salt Creek Valley, the most beautiful valley I have ever seen. In this valley lay our future home.

The hill was very steep, and I remember we had to "lock" or chain the wagon-wheels as we descended. We made camp in the valley. The next day father began trading with the Indians, who were so pleased with the bargains he had to offer that they sent their friends back to us when they departed.

One of the first trades he made was for a little pony for me—a four-year-old—which I was told I should have to break myself. I named him Prince. I had a couple of hard falls, but I made up my mind I was going to ride that pony or bust, and—I did not bust.

The next evening, looking over toward the west, I saw a truly frontier sight—a line of trappers winding down the hillside with their pack animals. My mother had often told me of the trappers searching the distant mountains for fur-bearing animals and living a life of fascinating adventure. Here they were in reality.

While some of the men prepared the skins, others built a fire and began to get a meal. I watched them cook the dried venison, and was filled with wonder at their method of making bread, which was to wrap the dough about a stick and hold it over the coals till it was ready to eat. You can imagine my rapture when one of them—a pleasant-faced youth—looked up, and catching sight of me, invited me to share the meal.

Boys are always hungry, but I was especially hungry for such a meal as that. After it was over I hurried to camp and told my father all that had passed. At his request I brought the young trapper who had been so kind to me over to our camp, and there he had a long talk with father, telling him of his adventures by land and sea in all parts of the world.

He said that he looked forward with great interest to his arrival in Weston, as he expected to meet an uncle, Elijah Cody. He had seen none of his people for many years.

"If Elijah Cody is your uncle, I am too," said my father. "You must be the long-lost Horace Billings."

Father had guessed right. Horace had wandered long ago from the Ohio home and none of his family knew of his whereabouts. He had been to South America and to California, joining a band of trappers on the Columbia River and coming with them back across the Plains.

When I showed him my pony he offered to help break him for me. With very little trouble he rode the peppery little creature this way and that, and at last when he circled back to camp I found the animal had been mastered.

In the days that followed Horace gave me many useful lessons as a horseman. He was the prettiest rider I had ever seen. There had been a stampede of horses from the Fort, and a reward of ten dollars a head had been offered for all animals brought in. That was easy money for Horace. I would gallop along at his side as he chased the fugitive horses. He had a long, plaited lariat which settled surely over the neck of the brute he was after. Then, putting a "della walt" on the pommel of his saddle, he would check his own mount and bring his captive to a sudden standstill. He caught and brought in five horses the first day, and must have captured twenty-five within the next few days, earning a sum of money which was almost a small fortune in that time.

Meanwhile the Territory had been opened for settlement. Our claim, over which the Great Salt Lake trail for California passed, had been taken up, and as soon as father and I, assisted by men he hired, could get our log cabin up, the family came on from Weston. The cabin was a primitive affair. There was no floor at first. But gradually we built a floor and partitions, and made it habitable. I spent all my spare time picking up the Kickapoo tongue from the Indian children in the neighborhood, and listening with both ears to the tales of the wide plains beyond.

The great freighting firm of Russell, Majors & Waddell was then sending its twenty-five wagon trains out from the Plains to carry supplies to the soldiers at the frontier forts. Leavenworth was the firm's headquarters. Russell stayed on the books, and Majors was the operating man on the Plains. The trains were wonderful to me, each wagon with its six yoke of oxen, wagon-masters, extra hands, assistants, bull-whackers and cavayard driver following with herds of extra oxen. I began at once making the acquaintance of the men, and by the end of 1854 I knew them all.

Up to this time, while bad blood existed between the Free-soilers and the pro-slavery men, it had not become a killing game. The pro-slavery Missourians were in the great majority. They harassed the Free-soilers considerably and committed many petty persecutions, but no blood was shed. Father's brother, Elijah, who kept the store at Weston, was known to be a pro-slavery man, and for a time it was taken for granted that father held the same views. But he was never at any pains to hide his own opinions, being a man who was afraid of nothing. John Brown of Ossawatomie, later hanged, for the Harper's Ferry raid, at Charlestown, Va., was his friend. So were Colonel Jim Lane and many other Abolitionists. He went to their houses openly, and they came to his. He worked hard with the men he had hired, cutting the wild hay and cordwood to sell to the Fort, and planting sod corn under the newly turned sod of the farm. He also made a garden, plowing and harrowing the soil and breaking up the sods by hitching horses to branching trees and drawing them over the ground. He minded his own business and avoided all the factional disputes with which the neighborhood abounded.

In June, 1856, when I was ten years old, father went to the Fort to collect his pay for hay and wood he had sold there. I accompanied him on my pony. On our return we saw a crowd of drunken horsemen in front of Riveley's trading-post—as stores were called on the frontier. There were many men in the crowd and they were all drunk, yelling and shooting their pistols in the air. They caught sight of us immediately and a few of them advanced toward us as we rode up. Father expected trouble, but he was not a man to turn back. We rode quietly up to them, and were about to continue on past when one of them yelled:

"There's that abolition cuss now. Git him up here and make him declar' hisself!"

"Git off that hoss, Cody!" shouted another.

By this time more than a dozen men were crowding about father, cursing and abusing him. Soon they tore him from his horse. One of them rolled a drygoods box from the store.

"Now," he said, "git up on that thar box, and tell us whar' ye stand."

Standing on the box, father looked at the ringleaders with no sign of fear.

"I am not ashamed of my views," he said, quietly. "I am not an Abolitionist, and never have been. I think it is better to let slavery alone in the States where it is now. But I am not at all afraid to tell you that I am opposed to its extension, and that I believe that it should be kept out of Kansas."

His speech was followed by a wild yell of derision. Men began crowding around him, cursing and shaking their fists. One of them, whom I recognized as Charlie Dunn, an employee of my Uncle Elijah, worked his way through the crowd, and jumped up on the box directly behind father. I saw the gleam of a knife. The next instant, without a groan, father fell forward stabbed in the back. Somehow I got off my pony and ran to his assistance, catching him as he fell. His weight overbore me but I eased him as he came to the ground.

Dunn was still standing, knife in hand, seeking a chance for another thrust.

"Look out, ye'll stab the kid!" somebody yelled. Another man, with a vestige of decency, restrained the murderer. Riveley came out of the store. There was a little breaking up of the crowd. Dunn was got away. What happened to him later I shall tell you in another chapter.

With the help of a friend I got father into a wagon, when the crowd had gone. I held his head in my lap during the ride home. I believed he was mortally wounded. He had been stabbed down through the kidneys, leaving an ugly wound. But he did not die of it—then. Mother nursed him carefully and had he been spared further persecution, he might have survived. But this was only the beginning.

The pro-slavers waited a few days, and finding there was no move to molest them, grew bold. They announced that they were coming to our house to finish their work.

One night we heard that a party was organized to carry out this purpose. As quietly as possible mother helped take father out into the sod corn, which then grew tall and thick close about the cabin. She put a shawl round him and a sun-bonnet on his head to disguise him as he was taken out.

There in the sod corn we made him a bed of hay and blankets and there we kept him for days, carrying food to him by night. These were anxious days for my mother and her little family. My first real work as a scout began then, for I had to keep constantly on the watch for raids by the ruffians, who had now sworn that father must die.

As soon as he was able to walk we decided that he must be got away. Twenty-five miles distant, at Grasshopper Falls, were a party of his friends. There he hoped one day to plant a colony. With the help of a few friends we moved him thither one night, but word of his whereabouts soon reached his enemies.

I kept constantly on the alert, and, hearing that a party had set out to murder him at the Falls, I got into the saddle and sped out to warn him.

At a ford on the way I ran into the gang, who had stopped to water their horses.

As I galloped past, one of them yelled: "There's Cody's kid now on his way to warn his father. Stop, you, and tell us where your old man is."

A pistol shot, to terrify me into obedience, accompanied the command. I may have been terrified, but it was not into obedience. I got out of there like a shot, and though they rode hard on my trail my pony was too fast for them. My warning was in time.

We got father as quickly as we could to Lawrence, which was an abolition stronghold, and where he was safe for the time being. He gradually got back a part of his strength, enough of it at any rate to enable him to take part in the repulse of a raid of Missourians who came over to burn Lawrence and lynch the Abolitionists. They were driven back across the Missouri River by the Lawrence men, who trapped them into an ambush and so frightened them that for the present they rode on their raids no more.

When father returned to Salt Creek Valley the persecutions began again. The gangsters drove off all our stock and killed all our pigs and even the chickens. One night Judge Sharpe, a disreputable old alcoholic who had been elected a justice of the peace, came to the house and demanded a meal. Mother, trembling for the safety of her husband, who lay sick upstairs, hastened to get it for him. As the old scoundrel sat waiting he caught sight of me.

"Look yere, kid," he shouted, "ye see this knife?"

He drew a long, wicked bowie. "Well, I'm going to sharpen that to finish up the job that Charlie Dunn began the other day." And scowling horribly at me he began whetting the knife on a stone he picked up from the table.

Now, I knew something about a gun, and there was a gun handy. It was upstairs, and I lost no time in getting it. Sitting on the stairs I cocked it and held it across my knees. I am sure that I should have shot him had he attempted to come up those stairs.

He didn't test my shooting ability, however. He got even with me by taking my beloved pony, Prince, when he left. Mother pleaded with him to leave it, for it was the only animal we had, but she might as well have pleaded with a wildcat.

We had now been reduced to utter destitution. Our only food was what rabbits and birds I could trap and catch with the help of our faithful old dog Turk, and the sod corn which we grated into flour. Father could be of no service to us. His presence, in fact, was merely a menace. So, with the help of Brown, Jim Lane and other Free-soilers, he made his way back to Ohio and began recruiting for his Grasshopper Falls colony.

He returned to us in the spring of '57 mortally ill. The wound inflicted by Dunn had at last fulfilled the murderer's purpose. Father died in the little log-house, the first man to shed his blood in the fight against the extension of slavery into the Northern Territories.

I was eleven years old, and the only man of the family. I made up my mind to be a breadwinner.

At that time the Fort was full of warlike preparations. A great number of troops were being assembled to send against the Mormons. Trouble had been long expected. United States Judges and Federal officers sent to the Territory of Utah had been flouted. Some of them never dared take their seats. Those who did asked assistance. Congress at last decided to give it to them. General Harney was to command the expedition. Col. Albert Sidney Johnston, afterward killed at Shiloh, where he fought on the Confederate side, was in charge of the expedition to which the earliest trains were to be sent.

Many of the soldiers had already pushed on ahead. Russell, Majors & Waddell were awarded the contract for taking them supplies and beef cattle. The supplies were forwarded in the long trains of twenty-five wagons, of which I have told you. The cattle were driven after the soldiers, the herds often falling many miles behind them.

I watched these great preparations eagerly, and it occurred to me that I ought to have a share in them. I went to Mr. Majors, whom I always called Uncle Aleck, and asked him for a job. I told him of our situation, and that I needed it very badly for the support of my mother and family.

"But you're only a boy, Billy," he objected. "What can you do?"

"I can ride as well as a man," I said. "I could drive cavayard, couldn't I?" Driving cavayard is herding the extra cattle that follow the wagon train.

Mr. Majors agreed that I could do this, and consented to employ me. I was to receive a man's wages, forty dollars a month and food, and the wages were to be paid to my mother while I was gone. With forty dollars a month she would be able to support her daughters and my baby brother in comfort. Before I was allowed to go to work Uncle Aleck handed me the oath which every one of his employees must sign. I did my best to live up to its provisions, but I am afraid that the profanity clause at least was occasionally violated by some of the bull-whackers. Here is the oath:

"We, the undersigned wagon-masters, assistants, teamsters and all other employees of the firm of Russell, Majors & Waddell, do hereby sign that we will not swear, drink whisky, play cards or be cruel to dumb beasts in any way, shape or form.

X (his mark)

(Signed) "WILLIAM FREDERICK CODY."

I signed it with my mark, for I could not write then. After administering this ironclad oath Mr. Majors gave each man a Testament.

My first job was that of accompanying a herd of cattle destined for beef for the troops that had gone on ahead. Bill McCarthy, boss of the outfit, was a typical Westerner, rough but courageous, and with plenty of experience on the frontier.

We progressed peacefully enough till we made Plum Creek, thirty-six miles west of Fort Kearney, on the South Platte. The trip had been full of excitement for me. The camp life was rough, the bacon often rusty and the flour moldy, but the hard work gave us big appetites. Plainsmen learn not to be particular.

I remember that on some of our trips we obtained such "luxuries" as dried apples and beans as part of our supplies. We could only have these once every two or three days, and their presence in the mess was always a glad occasion.

We were nooning at Plum Creek, the cattle spread out over the prairie to graze in charge of two herders. Suddenly there was a sharp Bang! Bang! Bang! and a thunder of hoofs.

"Indians! They've shot the herders and stampeded the cattle!" cried McCarthy. "Get under the banks of the river, boys—use 'em for a breastwork!"

We obeyed orders quickly. The Platte, a wide, shallow, muddy stream, flows under banks which vary from five to thirty feet in height. Behind them we were in much the position of European soldiers in a trench. We had our guns, and if the Indians showed over the bank could have made it hot for them.

McCarthy told us to keep together and to make our way down the river to Fort Kearney, the nearest refuge. It was a long and wearying journey, but our lives depended on keeping along the river bed. Often we would have to wade the stream which, while knee-deep to the men, was well-nigh waist-deep to me. Gradually I fell behind, and when night came I was dragging one weary step after another—dog-tired but still clinging to my old Mississippi Yaeger rifle, a short muzzle-loader which carried a ball and two buckshot.

Darkness came, and I still toiled along. The men ahead were almost out of hearing. Presently the moon rose, dead ahead of me. And painted boldly across its face was the black figure of an Indian. There could be no mistaking him for a white man. He wore the war-bonnet of the Sioux, and at his shoulder was a rifle, pointed at someone in the bottom below him. I knew well enough that in another second he would drop one of my friends. So I raised my Yaeger and fired. I saw the figure collapse, and heard it come tumbling thirty feet down the bank, landing with a splash in the water.

McCarthy and the rest of the party, hearing the shot, came back in a hurry. "What is it?" asked McCarthy, when he came up to me.

"I don't know," I said. "Whatever it is, it is down there in the water."

McCarthy ran over to the brave. "Hi!" he cried. "Little Billy's killed an Indian all by himself!"

Not caring to meet any of this gentleman's friends we pushed on still faster toward Fort Kearney, which we reached about daylight. We were given food and sent to bed, while the soldiers set out to look for our slain comrades and to try to recover our cattle.

Soldiers from Fort Leavenworth found the herders, killed and mutilated in the Indian fashion. But the cattle had been stampeded among the buffalo and it was impossible to recover a single head.

We were taken back to Leavenworth on one of the returning freight wagon-trains. The news of my exploit was noised about and made me the envy of all the boys of the neighborhood. The LeavenworthTimes, published by D.B. Anthony, sent a reporter to get the story of the adventure, and in it my name was printed for the first time as the youngest Indian slayer of the Plains.

I was persuaded now that I was destined to lead a life on the Plains. The two months that our ill-fated expedition had consumed had not discouraged me. Once more I applied to Mr. Majors for a job.

"You seem to have a reputation as a frontiersman, Billy," he said; "I guess I'll have to give yon another chance." He turned me over to Lew Simpson, who was boss of a twenty-five wagon-train just starting with supplies for General Albert Sidney Johnston's army, which was then on its way to Great Salt Lake to fight the Mormons, whose Destroying Angels, or Danites, were engaged in many outrages on Gentile immigrants.

Simpson appeared to be glad to have me. "We need Indian fighters, Billy," he told me, and giving me a mule to ride assigned me to a job as cavayard driver.

Our long train, twenty-five wagons in a line, each with its six yoke of oxen, rolled slowly out of Leavenworth over the western trail. Wagon-master assistants, bull-whackers—thirty men in all not to mention the cavayard driver—it was an imposing sight. This was to be a long journey, clear to the Utah country, and I eagerly looked forward to new adventures.

The first of these came suddenly. We were strung out over the trail near the Platte, about twenty miles from the scene of the Indian attack on McCarthy's outfit, watching the buffalo scattered to right and left of us, when we heard two or three shots, fired in rapid succession.

Before we could find out who fired them, down upon us came a herd of buffalo, charging in a furious stampede. There was no time to do anything but jump behind our wagons. The light mess-wagon was drawn by six yoke of Texas steers which instantly became part of the stampede, tearing away over the prairie with the buffalo, our wagon following along behind. The other wagons were too heavy for the steers to gallop away with; otherwise the whole outfit would have gone.

I remember that one big bull came galloping down between two yoke of oxen, tearing away the gooseneck and the heavy chain with each lowered horn. I can still see him as he rushed away with these remarkable decorations dangling from either side. Whether or not his new ornaments excited the admiration of his fellows when the herd came to a stand later in the day, I can only guess.

The descent of the buffalo upon us lasted only a few minutes, but so much damage was done that three days were required to repair it before we could move on. We managed to secure our mess-wagon, again, which was lucky, for it contained all our provender.

We learned afterward that the stampede had been caused by a returning party of California gold-seekers, whose shots into the herd had been our first warning of what was coming. Twice before we neared the Mormon country we were attacked by Indians. The army was so far ahead that they had become bold. We beat off the attacks, but lost two men.

It was white men, however, not Indians, who were to prove our most dangerous enemies. Arriving near Green River we were nooning on a ridge about a mile and a half from a little creek, Halm's Fork, where the stock were driven to water. This was a hundred and fifteen miles east of Salt Lake City, and well within the limits of the Mormon country.

Most of the outfit had driven the cattle to the creek, a mile and a half distant, and were returning slowly, while the animals grazed along the way back to camp. I was with them. We were out of sight of the wagons.

As we rose the hill a big bearded man, mounted and surrounded by a party of armed followers, rode up to our wagon-master.

"Throw up your hands, Simpson!" said the leader, who knew Simpson's name and his position.

Simpson was a brave man, but the strangers had the drop and up went his hands. At the same time we saw that the wagons were surrounded by several hundred men, all mounted and armed, and the teamsters all rounded up in a bunch. We knew that we had fallen into the hands of the Mormon Danites, or Destroying Angels, the ruffians who perpetrated the dreadful Mountain Meadows Massacre of the same year. The leader was Lot Smith, one of the bravest and most determined of the whole crowd.

"Now, Simpson," he said, "we are going to be kind to you. You can have one wagon with the cattle to draw it. Get into it all the provisions and blankets you can carry, and turn right round and go back to the Missouri River. You're headed in the wrong direction."

"Can we have our guns?" asked Simpson. "Not a gun."

"Six-shooters?"

"Not a six-shooter. Nothing but food and blankets." "How are we going to protect ourselves on the way?"

"That's your business. We're doing you a favor to spare your lives."

All Simpson's protests were in vain. There were thirty of us against several hundred of them. Mormons stood over us while we loaded a wagon till it sagged with provisions, clothing and blankets. They had taken away every rifle and every pistol we possessed. Ordering us to hike for the East, and informing us that we would be shot down if we attempted to turn back, they watched us depart.

When we had moved a little way off we saw a blaze against the sky behind us, and knew that our wagon-train had been fired. The greasy bacon made thick black smoke and a bright-red flame, and for a long time the fire burned, till nothing was left but the iron bolts and axles and tires.

Smith's party, which had been sent out to keep all supplies from reaching Johnston's army, had burned two other wagon-trains that same day, as we afterward learned. The wagons were all completely consumed, and for the next few years the Mormons would ride out to the scenes to get the iron that was left in the ashes.

Turned adrift on the desert with not a weapon to defend ourselves was hardly a pleasant prospect. It meant a walk of a thousand miles home to Leavenworth. The wagon was loaded to its full capacity. There was nothing to do but walk. I was not yet twelve years old, but I had to walk with the rest the full thousand miles, and we made nearly thirty miles a day.

Fortunately we were not molested by Indians. From passing wagon-trains we got a few rifles, all they could spare, and with these we were able to kill game for fresh meat. I wore out three pairs of moccasins on that journey, and learned then that the thicker are the soles of your shoes, the easier are your feet on a long walk over rough ground.

After a month of hard travel we reached Leavenworth. I set out at once for the log-cabin home, whistling as I walked, and the first to welcome me was my old dog Turk, who came tearing toward me and almost knocked me down in his eagerness. I am sure my mother and sisters were mighty glad to see me. They had feared that I might never return.

My next journey over the Plains was begun under what, to me, were very exciting circumstances. I spent the winter of '57-'58 at school. My mother was anxious about my education. But the master of the frontier school wore out several armfuls of hazel switches in a vain effort to interest me in the "three R's."

I kept thinking of my short but adventurous past. And as soon as another opportunity offered to return to it I seized it eagerly.

That spring my former boss, Lew Simpson, was busily organizing a "lightning bull team" for his employers, Russell, Majors & Waddell. Albert Sidney Johnston's soldiers, then moving West, needed supplies, and needed them in a hurry. Thus far the mule was the reindeer of draft animals, and mule trains were forming to hurry the needful supplies to the soldiers.

But Simpson had great faith in the bull. A picked bull train, he allowed, could beat a mule train all hollow on a long haul. All he wanted was a chance to prove it.

His employers gave him the chance. For several weeks he had

been picking his animals for the outfit. And now he was to begin what is perhaps the most remarkable race ever made across the Plains.

A mule train was to start a week after Simpson's lightning bulls began their westward course. Whichever outfit got to Fort Laramie first would be the winner. No more excitement could have been occasioned had the contestants been a reindeer and a jack-rabbit. To my infinite delight Simpson let me join his party.

My thousand-mile tramp over the Plains had cured me of the walking habit and I was glad to find that this time I was to have a horse to ride—part of the way, anyhow. I was to be an extra hand—which meant that by turns I was to be a bull-whacker, driver and general-utility man.

I remember that our start was a big event. Men, women and children watched our chosen animals amble out of Salt Creek. The "mule skinners," busy with preparations for their own departure, stopped work to jeer us.

"We'll ketch you in a couple of days or so!" yelled Tom Stewart, boss of the mule outfit.

But Simpson only grinned. Jeers couldn't shake his confidence either in himself or his long-horned motive power.

We made the first hundred and fifty miles easily. I was glad to be a plainsman once more, and took a lively interest in everything that went forward. We were really making speed, too, which added to the excitement. The ordinary bull team could do about fifteen miles a day. Under Simpson's command his specially selected bulls were doing twenty-five, and doing it right along.

But one day, while we were nooning about one hundred and fifty miles on the way, one of the boys shouted: "Here come the mules!"

Presently Stewart's train came shambling up, and a joyful lot the "mule skinners" were at what they believed their victory.

But it was a short-lived victory. At the end of the next three hundred miles we found them, trying to cross the Platte, and making heavy work of it. The grass fodder had told on the mules. Supplies from other sources were now exhausted. There were no farms, no traders, no grain to be had. The race had become a race of endurance, and the strongest stomachs were destined to be the winners.

Stewart made a bad job of the crossing. The river was high, and his mules quickly mired down in the quicksand. The more they pawed the deeper they went.

Simpson picked a place for crossing below the ford Stewart had chosen. He put enough bulls on a wagon to insure its easy progress, and the bulls wallowed through the sand on their round bellies, using their legs as paddles.

Steward pulled ahead again after he had crossed the river, but soon his mules grew too feeble to make anything like their normal speed. We passed them for good and all a few days farther on, and were far ahead when we reached the North Platte.

Thus ended a race that I shall never forget. Since that time the stage-coach has outdistanced the bull team, the pony express has swept past the stage-coach, the locomotive has done in an hour what the prairie schooner did in three or four days. Soon the aeroplane will be racing with the automobile for the cross-country record.

But the bull team and the mule team were the continental carriers of that day, and I am very glad that I took part—on the winning side—in a race between them.

We soon began meeting parties of soldiers, and lightening

our loads by issuing supplies to them. When at last we reacted Fort Laramie, the outfit was ordered to Fort Walback, located in Cheyenne Pass, twenty-five miles from where Cheyenne stands today, and ninety miles from Fort Laramie.

This was in the very heart of the Indian country. Our animals were to haul in plows, tools and whatever was necessary in the constructing of the new fort then building. The wagon-beds were taken from the wagons to enable the hauling of greater loads. The beds were piled up at Fort Laramie, and I was assigned to watch them. It was here that I had abundant time and opportunity to study the West at first hand. Heretofore I had been on the march. Now I was on fixed post with plenty of time for observation.

Fort Laramie was an old frontier post, such as has not existed for many years. Nearby, three or four thousand Sioux, Northern Cheyennes and Northern Arapahoes were encamped, most of them spending much of the time at the post. Laramie had been established by a fur-trading company in 1834. In 1840 or thereabouts the Government bought it and made it a military post. It had become the most famous meeting-place of the Plains. Here the greatest Indian councils were held, and here also came the most celebrated of the Indian fighters, men whose names had long been known to me, but whom I never dared hope to see.

Kit Carson, Jim Bridger, Baker, Richards and other of the celebrated hunters, trappers and Indian fighters were as familiar about the post as are bankers in Wall Street. All these men fascinated me, especially Carson, a small, dapper, quiet man whom everybody held in profound respect.

I used to sit for hours and watch him and the others talk to the Indians in the sign language. Without a sound they would carry on long and interesting conversations, tell stories, inquire about game and trails, and discuss pretty much everything that men find worth discussing. I was naturally desirous of mastering this mysterious medium of speech, and began my education in it with far more interest than I had given to the "three R's" back at Salt Creek. My wagon-beds became splendid playhouses for the Indian children from the villages, who are very much like other children, despite their red skins.

I joined them in their games, and from them picked up a fair working knowledge of the Sioux language. The acquaintance I formed here was to save my scalp and life later, but I little suspected it then.

I spent the summer of '58 in and about Laramie. I was getting to be a big, husky boy now, and felt that I had entered on what was to be my career—as indeed I had.

In January, '59, Simpson was ordered back to Missouri as brigade train- master of three wagon-trains, traveling a day apart. Because of much travel the grass along the regular trail was eaten so close that the feed for the bulls was scanty.

Instead of following the trail down the South Platte, therefore, Simpson picked a new route along the North Platte. There was no road, but the grass was still long, and forage for the cattle was necessary.

We had accomplished about half our journey with no sign of hostile Indians. Then one day, as Simpson, George Woods and I were riding ahead to overtake the lead train, a party of Sioux bore down on us, plainly intent on mischief. There was little time to act. No cover of any kind was to be had.

For us three, even with our rifles, to have stood up against the Sioux in the open would have been suicide. Simpson had been trained to think quickly. Swinging the three mules so that they formed a triangle, he drew his six- shooter and dropped them where they stood.

"Now there's a little cover, boys," he said, and we all made ready for the attack.

Our plan of defense was now made for us. First rifles, then, at closer quarters, revolvers. If it came to a hand-to-hand conflict we had our knives as a last resort.

The Sioux drew up when they saw how quickly Simpson's wit had built a barricade for us. Then the arrows began to fly and among them spattered a few bullets. We were as sparing as possible with our shots. Most of them told. I had already learned how to use a rifle, and was glad indeed that I had. If ever a boy stood in need of that kind of preparedness I did.

Down came the Indians, with the blood-curdling yell which is always a feature of their military strategy. We waited till they got well within range. Then at Simpson's order we fired. Three ponies galloped riderless over the prairie, and our besiegers hesitated, then wheeled, and rode out of range. But our rest was short. Back they came. Again we fired, and had the good fortune to stop three more of them.

Simpson patted me encouragingly on the shoulder. "You're all right, Billy!" he said, and his praise was music to my ears.

By this time our poor dead mules, who had given their lives for ours, were stuck full of arrows. Woods had been winged in the shoulder. Simpson, carefully examining the wound, expressed his belief that the arrow which inflicted it had not been poisoned.

But we had little time to worry about that or anything else. Our enemies were still circling, just out of range. Here and there when they grew incautious we dropped a man or a pony. But we were still heavily outnumbered. They knew it and we knew it. Unless help came it was only a question of time till it was all over.

Daylight came and they still held off. Eagerly we looked to

the westward, but no wagon-train appeared. We began to fear that something had happened to our friends, when, suddenly one of the Indians jumped up, and with every evidence of excitement signaled to the others. In an instant they were all mounted.

"They hear the crack of the bull-whip," said Woods.

He was right. Without another glance in our direction the Sioux galloped away toward the foot-hills, and as they disappeared we heard the welcome snap of the long bull-whip, and saw the first of our wagons coming up the trail. In that day, however, the plainsman was delivered out of one peril only to be plunged into another. His days seldom dragged for want of excitement.

When we got to Leavenworth, Simpson sent three of us ahead with the train-book record of the men's time, so that their money would be ready for them when they arrived at Leavenworth.

Our boss's admonition to ride only at night and to lie under cover in daytime was hardly needed. We cared for no more Indian adventures just then.

We made fairly good progress till we got to the Little Blue, in Colorado. It was an uncomfortable journey, finding our way by the stars at night and lying all day in such shelters as were to be found. But the inconvenience of it was far preferable to being made targets for Indian arrows.

We were sheltered one night from one of the fearful prairie blizzards that make fall and winter terrible. We had found a gulley washed out by an autumn storm, and it afforded a little protection against the wind. Looking down the ravine I saw ponies moving. I knew there were Indians near, and we looked about for a hiding-place.

At the head of the ravine I had noticed a cave-like hollow. I signaled to the two men to follow me, and soon we were snug in a safe hiding-place. As we were settling down to rest one of the men lit his pipe. As the cave was illuminated by the glow of the match there was a wild yell. I thought all the Indians in the world had jumped us. But the yell had come from my companions.

We were in the exact center of the most grew-some collection of human skulls and bones I have ever seen. Bones were strewn on the floor of the cave like driftwood. Skulls were grinning at us from every corner of the darkness. We had stumbled into a big grave where some of the Indians had hidden their dead away from the wolves after a battle. It may be that none of us were superstitious, but we got out of there in a hurry, and braved the peril of the storm and the Indians as best we could.

I was a rich boy when I got to Leavenworth. I had nearly a thousand dollars to turn over to my mother as soon as I should draw my pay. After a joyful reunion with the family I hitched up a pair of ponies, and drove her over so that she could witness this pleasing ceremony. As we were driving home, I heard her sobbing, and was deeply concerned, for this seemed to me no occasion for tears. I was quick to ask the reason, and her answer made me serious.

"You couldn't even write your name, Willie," she said. "You couldn't sign the payroll. To think my boy cannot so much as write his name!"

I thought that over all the way home, and determined it should never happen again.

In Uncle Aleck Majors' book, "Seventy Years on the Frontier," he relates how on every wagon-sheet and wagon-bed, on every tree and barn door, he used to find the name "William F. Cody" in a large, uncertain scrawl. Those were my writing lessons, and

I took them daily until I had my signature plastered pretty well over the whole of Salt Creek Valley.

I went to school for a time after that, and at last began really to take an interest in education. But the Pike's Peak gold rush took me with it. I could never resist the call of the trail. With another boy who knew as little of gold-mining as I did we hired out with a bull-train for Denver, then called Aurora.

We each had fifty dollars when we got to the gold country, and with it we bought an elaborate outfit. But there was no mining to be done save by expensive machinery, and we had our labor for our pains. At last, both of us strapped, we got work as timber cutters, which lasted only until we found it would take us a week to fell a tree. At last we hired out once more as bull-whackers. That job we understood, and at it we earned enough money to take us home.

We hired a carpenter to build us a boat, loaded it with grub and supplies, and started gayly down the Platte for home. But the bad luck of that trip held steadily. The boat was overturned in swift and shallow water, and we were stranded, wet and helpless, on the bank, many miles from home or anywhere else.

Then a miracle happened. Along the trail we heard the familiar crack of a bull-whip, and when the train came up we found it was the same with which we had enlisted for the outward journey, returning to Denver with mining machinery. Among this machinery was a big steam-boiler, the first to be taken into Colorado. On the way out the outfit had been jumped by Indians. The wagon boss, knowing the red man's fear of cannon, had swung the great boiler around so that it had appeared to point at them. Never was so big a cannon. Even the 42-centimeter howitzers of today could not compare with it. The Indians took one look at it, then departed that part of the country as fast as their ponies could travel.

We stuck with the train into Denver and back home again, and glad we were to retire from gold-mining.

Soon after my return to Salt Creek Valley I decided on another and, I thought, a better way to make a fortune for myself and my family.

During my stay in and about Fort Laramie I had seen much of the Indian traders, and accompanied them on a number of expeditions. Their business was to sell to the Indians various things they needed, chiefly guns and ammunition, and to take in return the current Indian coin, which consisted of furs.

With the supplies bought by the money I had earned on the trip with Simpson, mother and my sisters were fairly comfortable. I felt that I should be able to embark in the fur business on my own account—not as a trader but as a trapper.

With my friend Dave Harrington as a companion I set out. Harrington was older than I, and had trapped before in the Rockies. I was sure that with my knowledge of the Plains and his of the ways of the fur-bearing animals, we should form an excellent partnership, as in truth we did.

We bought a yoke of oxen, a wagon-sheet, wagon, traps of all sorts, and strychnine with which to poison wolves. Also we laid in a supply of grub—no luxuries, but coffee, flour, bacon and everything that we actually needed to sustain life.

We headed west, and about two hundred miles from home we struck Prairie Creek, where we found abundant signs of beaver, mink, otter and other fur-bearing animals. No Indians had troubled us, and we felt safe in establishing headquarters here and beginning work. The first task was to build a dugout in a hillside, which we roofed with brush, long grass, and finally dirt, making everything snug and cozy. A little fireplace in the wall served as both furnace and kitchen. Outside we built a corral for the oxen, which completed our camp.

Our trapping was successful from the start, and we were sure that prosperity was at last in sight.

We set our steel traps along the "runs" used by the animals, taking great care to hide our tracks, and give the game no indication of the presence of an enemy. The pelts began to pile up in our shack. Most of the day we were busy at the traps, or skinning and salting the hides, and at night we would sit by our little fire and swap experiences till we fell asleep. Always there was the wail of the coyotes and the cries of other animals without, but as long as we saw no Indians we were not worried.

One night, just as we were dozing off, we heard a tremendous commotion in the corral. Harrington grabbed his gun and hurried out. He was just in time to see a big bear throw one of our oxen and proceed with the work of butchering him.

He fired, and the bear, slightly wounded, left the ox and turned his attention to his assailant. He was leaping at my partner, growling savagely when I, gun in hand, rounded the corner of the shack. I took the best aim I could get in the dark, and the bear, which was within a few feet of my friend, rolled over dead.

Making sure that he was past harming us we turned our attention to the poor bull, but he was too far gone to recover, and another bullet put him out of his misery.

We were now left without a team, and two hundred miles from home. But wealth in the shape of pelts was accumulating about us, and we determined to stick it out till spring. Then one of us could go to the nearest settlement for a teammate for our remaining steer, while the other stayed in charge of the camp.

This plan had to be carried out far sooner than we expected. A few days later we espied a herd of elk, which meant plentiful and excellent meat. We at once started in pursuit. Creeping stealthily along toward them, keeping out of sight, and awaiting an opportunity to get a good shot, I slipped on a stone in the creek bed.

"Snap!" went something and looking down I saw my foot hanging useless. I had broken my leg just above the ankle and my present career as a fur- trapper had ended.

I was very miserable when Harrington came up. I urged him to shoot me as he had thc ox, but he laughingly replied that that would hardly do.

"I'll bring you out all right!" he said. "I owe you a life anyway for saving me from that bear. I learned a little something about surgery when I was in Illinois, and I guess I can fix you up."

He got me back to camp after a long and painful hour and with a wagon- bow, which he made into a splint, set the fracture. But our enterprise was at an end. Help would have to be found now, and before spring. One man and a cripple could never get through the winter.

It was determined that Harrington must go for this needful assistance just as soon as possible. He placed me on our little bunk, with plenty of blankets to cover me. All our provisions he put within my reach. A cup was lashed to a long sapling, and Harrington made a hole in the side of the dugout so that I could reach this cup out to a snow-bank for my water supply.

Lastly he cut a great pile of wood and heaped it near the fire. Without leaving the bunk I could thus do a little cooking, keep the fire up, and eat and sleep. It was not a situation that I would have chosen, but there was nothing else to do.

The nearest settlement was a hundred and twenty-five miles distant. Harrington figured that he could make the round trip in twenty days. My supplies were ample to last that long. I urged him to start as soon as possible, that he might the sooner return with a new yoke of oxen. Then I could be hauled out to where medical attendance was to be had.

I watched him start off afoot, and my heart was heavy. But soon I stopped thinking of my pain and began to find ways and means to cure my loneliness. We had brought with us a number of books, and these I read through most of my waking hours. But the days grew longer and longer for all that. Every morning when I woke I cut a notch in a long stick to mark its coming. I had cut twelve of these notches when one morning I was awakened from a sound sleep by the touch of a hand on my shoulder.

Instantly concluding that Harrington had returned, I was about to cry out in delight when I caught a glimpse of a war-bonnet, surmounting the ugly, painted face of a Sioux brave.

The brilliant colors that had been smeared on his visage told me more forcibly than words could have done that his tribe was on the warpath. It was a decidedly unpleasant discovery for me.

While he was asking me in the Sioux language what I was doing there, and how many more were in the party, other braves began crowding through the door till the little dugout was packed as full of Sioux warriors as it could hold.

Outside I could hear the stamping of horses and the voices of more warriors. I made up my mind it was all over but the scalping.

And then a stately old brave worked his way through the crowd and came toward my bunk. It was plain from the deference accorded him by the others that he was a chief. And as soon as I set eyes on him I recognized him as old Rain-in-the-Face, whom

I had often seen and talked with at Fort Laramie, and whose children taught me the Sioux language as we played about the wagon-beds together. Among these children was the son who succeeded to the name of Rain-in-the-Face, and who years later, it is asserted, killed General George A. Custer in the massacre of the Little Big Horn.

I showed the chief my broken leg, and asked him if he did not remember me. He replied that he did. I asked him if he intended to kill the boy who had been his children's playmate. He consulted with his warriors, who had begun busily to loot the cabin. After a long parley the old man told me that my life would be spared, but my gun and pistol and all my provisions would be regarded as the spoils of the war.

Vainly I pointed out that he might as well kill me as leave me without food or the means to defend myself against wolves. He said that his young men had granted a great deal in consenting to spare my life. As for food, he pointed to the carcass of a deer that hung from the wall.

The next morning they mounted their ponies and galloped away. I was glad enough to see them go. I knew that my life had hung by a thread while I had been their involuntary host. Only my friendship with the children of old Rain- in-the-Face had saved me.

But, even with the Indians gone, I was in a desperate situation. As they had taken all my matches I had to keep the fire going continuously. This meant that I could not sleep long at a time, the lack of rest soon began to tell on me. I would cut slices from the deer carcass with my knife, and holding it over the fire with a long stick, cook it, eating it without salt. Coffee I must do without altogether.

The second day after the departure of the Indians a great snow fell. The drifts blocked the doorway and covered the windows. It lay to a depth of several feet on the roof over my head. My woodpile was covered by the snow that drifted in and it was with great difficulty that I could get enough wood to keep my little fire going. And on that fire depended my life. Worse than all these troubles was the knowledge that the heavy snow would be sure to delay Harrington.

I would lie there, day after day, a prey to all sorts of dark imaginings. I fancied him killed by Indians on the trail, or snowbound and starving on the Plains. Each morning my notches on my calendar stick were made. Gradually their number grew till at last the twentieth was duly cut. But no Harrington came.

The wolves, smelling meat within, had now begun to gather round in increasing numbers. They made the night hideous with their howlings, and pawed and scratched and dug at the snow by the doorway, determined to come in and make a meal of everything the dugout contained, myself included.

How I endured it I do not know. But the Plains teach men and boys fortitude. Many and many a time as I lay there I resolved that if I should ever be spared to go back to my home and friends, the frontier should know me no more.

It was on the twenty-ninth day, as marked on stick, when I had about given up hope, that I heard a cheerful voice shouting "Whoa!" and recognized it as the voice of Harrington. A criminal on the scafford with the noose about his neck and the trap sagging underneath his feet could not have welcomed a pardon more eagerly than I welcomed my deliverance out of this torture- chamber.

I could make no effort to open the door for him. But I found voice to answer him when he cried "Hello, Billy!" and in response to his question assured him that I was all right. He soon cleared a passageway through the snow, and stood beside me.

"I never expected to see you alive again," he said; "I had a terrible trip. I didn't think I should ever get through—caught in the snowstorm and laid up for three days. The cattle wandered away and I came within an ace of losing them altogether. When I got started again the snow was so deep I couldn't make much headway."

"Well, you're here," I said, giving him a hug.

Harrington had made a trip few men could have made. He had risked his life to save mine. All alone he had brought a yoke of oxen over a country where the trails were all obscured and the blinding snow made every added mile more perilous.

I was still unable to walk, and he had to do all the work of packing up for the trip home. In a few days he had loaded the pelts on board the wagon, covered it with the wagon-sheet we had used in the dugout, and made me a comfortable bed inside. We had three hundred beaver and one hundred otter skins to show for our work. That meant a lot of money when we should get them to the settlements.

On the eighth day of the journey home we reached a ranch on the Republican River, where we rested for a couple of days. Then we went on to the ranch where Harrington had obtained his cattle and paid for the yoke with twenty-five beaver skins, the equivalent of a hundred dollars in money.

At the end of twenty days' travel we reached Salt Creek Valley, where I was welcomed by my mother and sisters as one returned from the dead.

So grateful was my mother to Harrington for what he had done for me that she insisted on his making his home with us.

This he decided to do, and took charge of our farm. The next spring, this man, who had safely weathered the most perilous of journeys over the Plains, caught cold while setting out some trees and fell ill. We brought a doctor from Lawrence, and did everything in our power to save him, but in a week he died. The loss of a member of our own family could not have affected us more.

I was now in my fifteenth year and possessed of a growing appetite for adventure. A very few months had so dulled the memory of my sufferings in the dugout that I had forgotten all about my resolve to forsake the frontier forever. I looked about me for something new and still more exciting.

I was not long in finding it. In April, 1860, the firm of Russell, Majors & Waddell organized the wonderful "Pony Express," the most picturesque messenger-service that this country has ever seen. The route was from St. Joseph, Missouri, to Sacramento, California, a distance of two thousand miles, across the Plains, over a dreary stretch of sagebrush and alkali desert, and through two great mountain ranges.

The system was really a relay race against time. Stations were built at intervals averaging fifteen miles apart. A rider's route covered three stations, with an exchange of horses at each, so that he was expected at the beginning to cover close to forty-five miles—a good ride when one must average fifteen miles an hour.

The firm undertaking the enterprise had been busy for some time picking the best ponies to be had for money, and the lightest, most wiry and most experienced riders. This was a life that appealed to me, and I struck for a job. I was pretty young in years, but I had already earned a reputation for coming safe out of perilous adventures, and I was hired.

Naturally our equipment was the very lightest. The messages which we carried were written on the thinnest paper to be found.

These we carried in a waterproof pouch, slung under our arms. We wore only such clothing as was absolutely necessary.

The first trip of the Pony Express was made in ten days—an average of two hundred miles a day. But we soon began stretching our riders and making better time. Soon we shortened the time to eight days. President Buchanan's last Presidential message in December, 1860, was carried in eight days. President Lincoln's inaugural, the following March, took only seven days and seventeen hours for the journey between St. Joseph and Sacramento.

We soon got used to the work. When it became apparent to the men in charge that the boys could do better than forty-five miles a day the stretches were lengthened. The pay of the rider was from $100 to $125 a month. It was announced that the further a man rode the better would be his pay. That put speed and endurance into all of us.

Stern necessity often compelled us to lengthen our day's work even beyond our desires. In the hostile Indian country, riders were frequently shot. In such an event the man whose relief had been killed had to ride on to the next station, doing two men's ride. Road-agents were another menace, and often they proved as deadly as the Indians.

In stretching my own route I found myself getting further and further west. Finally I was riding well into the foothills of the Rockies. Still further west my route was pushed. Soon I rode from Red Buttes to Sweetwater, a distance of seventy-six miles. Road-agents and Indians infested this country. I never was quite sure when I started out when I should reach my destination, or whether I should never reach it at all.

One day I galloped into the station at Three Crossings to find that my relief had been killed in a drunken row the night before. There was no one to take his place. His route was eighty-five miles across country to the west. I had no time to think it over. Selecting a good pony out of the stables I was soon on my way.

I arrived at Rocky Ridge, the end of the new route, on schedule time, and turning back came on to Red Buttes, my starting-place. The round trip was 320 miles, and I made it in twenty-one hours and forty minutes.

Excitement was plentiful during my two years' service as a Pony Express rider. One day as I was leaving Horse Creek, a party of fifteen Indians jammed me in a sand ravine eight miles west of the station. They fired at me repeatedly, but my luck held, and I went unscathed. My mount was a California roan pony, the fastest in the stables. I dug the spurs into his sides, and, lying flat on his back, I kept straight on for Sweetwater Bridge eleven miles distant. A turn back to Horse Creek might have brought me more speedily to shelter, but I did not dare risk it.

The Indians came on behind, riding with all the speed they could put into their horses, but my pony drew rapidly ahead. I had a lead of two miles when I reached the station. There I found I could get no new pony. The stock-tender had been killed by the Indians during the night. All his ponies had been stolen and driven off. I kept on, therefore, to Plonts Station, twelve miles further along, riding the same pony—a ride of twenty-four miles on one mount. At Plonts I told the people what had happened at Sweetwater Bridge. Then, with a fresh horse, I finished my route without further adventure.

❒

# Chapter–2.

About the middle of September the Indians became very troublesome on the line of the stage along the Sweetwater, between Split Rock and Three Crossings. A stage had been robbed and two passengers killed outright. Lem Flowers, the driver, was badly wounded. The thievish redskins also drove stock repeatedly from the stations. They were continually lying in wait for passing stages and Pony Express riders. It was useless to keep the Express going until these depredations could be stopped. A lay-off of six weeks was ordered, and our time was our own.

While we were thus idle a party was organized to carry the war into the Indians' own country, and teach them that the white man's property must be let alone. This party I joined.

Stage-drivers, express-riders, stock-tenders and ranchmen, forty in number, composed this party. All were well armed; all were good shots, and brave, determined men. "Wild Bill" Hickock, another of the Western gunmen of whom I shall have something to tell later, was captain of the expedition. He had come recently to our division as a stage-driver and had the experience and courage necessary to that kind of leadership.

Twenty miles out from Sweetwater Bridge, at the head of Horse Creek, we found an Indian trail running north toward

Powder River. We could see that the horses had been recently shod, conclusive proof that they were our stolen stock. We pushed on as fast as we could along the trail to the Powder, thence down this stream to within forty miles of where old Fort Reno now stands. Farther on, at Crazy Woman's Fork, we saw evidence that another party had joined our quarry. The trail was newly made. The Indians could be hardly more than twenty-four hours ahead of us. And plainly there was a lot of them.

When we reached Clear Creek, another tributary of the Powder, we saw horses grazing on the opposite bank. Horses meant Indians. Never before had the redskins been followed so far into their own country. Not dreaming that they would be pursued they had failed to put out scouts.

We quickly got the "lay" of their camp, and held a council to decide on how to attack them. We knew that they outnumbered us three to one—perhaps more. Without strategy, all we would get for our long chase would be the loss of our scalps.

"Wild Bill," who did not know the meaning of fear, made our plan for us. We were to wait till nightfall, and then, after creeping up as close as possible on the camp, make a grand ride right through it, open a general fire upon them, and stampede their horses.

It was a plan that called for nerve, but we were full of spirit, and the more danger there was in an enterprise the more we relished it. At our captain's signal we rushed pell-mell through their camp. Had we dropped from the clouds the Indians could not have been more astonished. At the sound of our shots they scattered in every direction, yelling warnings to each other as they fled.

Once clear of the camp we circled to the south and came back to make sure that we had done a thorough job. A few parting shots stampeded the stragglers. Then, with one hundred captured ponies—most, if not all of them, stolen from the Express and State stations—we rode back to Sweetwater Bridge.

The recovered horses were placed on the road again, and the Express was resumed. Slade, who was greatly pleased with our exploit, now assigned me as special or supernumerary rider. Thereafter while I was with him I had a comparatively easy time of it, riding only now and then, and having plenty of opportunity for seeking after the new adventures in which I delighted.

Alf Slade, stage-line superintendent, frontiersman, and dare-devil fighting man, was one of the far-famed gunmen of the Plains. These were a race of men bred by the perils and hard conditions of Western life. They became man-killers first from stern necessity. In that day the man who was not quick on the trigger had little chance with the outlaws among whom he had to live. Slade and "Wild Bill," with both of whom I became closely associated, were men of nerve and courage. But both, having earned the reputation of gun-fighters, became too eager to live up to it. Eventually both became outlaws.

Slade, though always a dangerous man, and extremely rough in his manner, never failed to treat me with kindness. Sober, he was cool and self- possessed, but never a man to be trifled with. Drunk, he was a living fury.

His services to the company for which he worked were of high value. He was easily the best superintendent on the line. But his habit of man-killing at last resulted in his execution.

Another man who gained even greater notoriety than Slade was "Wild Bill" Hickock, a tall, yellow-haired giant who had done splendid service as a scout in the western sector of the Civil War.

"Wild Bill" I had known since 1857. He and I shared the

pleasure of walking a thousand miles to the Missouri River, after the bull-train in which we both were employed had been burned by Lot Smith, the Mormon raider.

Afterward we rode the Pony Express together.

While an express rider, Bill had the fight with the McCandless gang which will always form an interesting chapter in the history of the West.

Coming into his swing station at Rock Creek one day, Bill failed to arouse any one with his shouts for a fresh mount. This was a certain indication of trouble. It was the stock-tender's business to be on hand with a relief pony the instant the rider came in. The Pony Express did not tolerate delays.

Galloping into the yard, Bill dismounted and hurried to the stable. In the door he saw the stock-tender lying dead, and at the same instant a woman's screams rang from the cabin near by. Turning about, Bill found himself face to face with a ruffian who was rushing from the house, brandishing a six- shooter. He asked no questions, but pulled one of the two guns he carried and fired. No sooner had the man fallen, however, than a second, also armed, came out of the house. Hickock disposed of this fellow also, and then entered the place, where four others opened a fusillade on him.

Although the room was thick with smoke, and Bill had to use extreme care to avoid hitting the woman, who was screaming in the corner, he managed to kill two of his assailants with his revolvers and to ward off a blow with a rifle a third had leveled at him.

The blow knocked the weapon from his hand, but his knife was still left him, and with it he put the man with the rifle out of the way. His troubles were not at an end, however. Another man came climbing in the window to avenge his fellow gangsters. Bill reached for a rifle which lay on the floor and shot first.

When he took count a few minutes later he discovered that he had killed five men and wounded a sixth, who escaped in the thick of the fight.

The woman, who had been knocked unconscious by one of the desperadoes, was soon revived. She was the stock-tender's wife, and had been attacked the by gang as soon as they had slain her husband.

The passengers of the Overland stage, which rolled in as Bill was reviving the terrified woman, were given a view of Western life which none of them ever forgot.

Bill was the hero of the occasion, and a real hero he was, for probably never has a man won such a victory against such terrific odds in all the history of the war against the ruffians of the West.

It was at Springfield, Missouri, that Bill had his celebrated fight with Dave Tutt. The fight put an end to Tutt's career. I was a personal witness to another of his gun exploits, in which, though the chances were all against him, he protected his own life and incidentally his money. An inveterate poker player, he got into a game in Springfield with big players and for high stakes. Sitting by the table, I noticed that he seemed sleepy and inattentive. So I kept a close watch on the other fellows. Presently I observed that one of his opponents was occasionally dropping a card in his hat, which he held in his lap, until a number of cards had been laid away for future use in the game.

The pot had gone around several times and was steadily raised by some of the players, Bill staying right along, though he still seemed to be drowsy.

The bets kept rising. At last the man with the hatful of cards picked a hand out of his reserves, put the hat on his head and raised Bill two hundred dollars. Bill came back with a raise of two hundred, and as the other covered it he quietly shoved a pistol into his face and observed: "I am calling the hand that is in your hat!"

Gathering in the pot with his left hand, he held the pistol with his right and inquired if any of the players had any objections to offer. They hastened to reply that they had no objections whatever and we went away from there.

"Bill," I said, when we were well outside the place, "I had been noticing that fellow's play right along, but I thought you hadn't. I was going to get into the game myself if he beat you out of that money."

"Billy," replied Hickock, "I don't want you ever to learn it, but that is one of my favorite poker tricks. It always wins against crooked players."

Not all of the gunmen of the West began straight. Some of them—many, in fact—were thieves and murderers from the beginning. Such were the members of the McCandless gang, which Hickock disposed of so thoroughly. All along the stage route were robbers and man-killers far more vicious than the Indians. Very early in my career as a frontiersman I had an encounter with a party of these from which I was extremely fortunate to escape with my life.

I employed the leisure afforded me by my assignment as an extra rider in hunting excursions, in which I took a keen delight. I was returning home empty-handed from a bear hunt, when night overtook me in a lonely spot near a mountain stream. I had killed two sage-hens and built a little fire over which to broil them before my night's rest.

Suddenly I heard a horse whinny farther up the stream.

Thinking instantly of Indians, I ran quickly to my own horse to prevent him from answering the call, and thus revealing my presence.

Filled with uneasiness as to who and what my human neighbors might be, I resaddled my horse, and, leaving him tied where I could reach him in a hurry if need be, made my way upstream to reconnoiter. As I came around a bend I received an unpleasant shock. Not one horse, but fifteen horses, were grazing just ahead of me.

On the opposite side of the creek a light shone high up the mountain bank— a light from the window of a dugout. I drew near very cautiously till I came within, sound of voices within the place, and discovered that its occupants were conversing in my own language. That relieved me. I knew the strangers to be white men. I supposed them to be trappers, and, walking boldly to the door, I knocked.

Instantly the voices ceased. There ensued absolute silence for a space, and then came-whisperings, and sounds of men quietly moving about the dirt floor.

"Who's there?" called someone.

"A friend and a white man," I replied.

The door opened, and a big, ugly-looking fellow stood before me. "Come in," he ordered.

I accepted the invitation with hesitation, but there was nothing else to do. To retreat would have meant pursuit and probably death.

Eight of the most villainous-appearing ruffians I have ever set eyes upon sat about the dugout as I entered. Two of them I recognized at once as teamsters who had been employed by Simpson a few months before. Both had been charged with murdering a ranchman and stealing his horses.

Simpson had promptly discharged them, and it was supposed that they had left the country.

I gave them no sign of recognition. I was laying my plans to get out of there as speedily as possible. I was now practically certain that I had uncovered the hiding-place of a gang of horse-thieves who could have no possible reason to feel anything but hostility toward an honest man. The leader of the gang swaggered toward me and inquired menacingly:

"Where are you going, young man, and who's with you?"

"I am entirely alone," I returned. "I left Horseshoe Station this morning for a bear hunt. Not finding any bears, I was going to camp out till morning. I heard one of your horses whinnying, and came up to your camp."

"Where is your horse?"

"I left him down the creek."

They proposed going for the horse, which was my only means of getting rid of their unwelcome society. I tried strategy to forestall them.

"I'll go and get him," I said. "I'll leave my gun here."

This, I fancied, would convince them that I intended to return, but it didn't.

"Jim and I will go with you," said one of the thieves. "You can leave your gun here if you want to. You won't need it."

I saw that if I was to get away at all I would have to be extremely alert. These were old hands, and were not to be easily fooled. I felt it safer, however, to trust myself with two men than with six, so I volunteered to show the precious pair where I had left the horse, and led them to my camp.

The animal was secured, and as one of the men started to lead him up the stream I picked up the two sage-hens I had intended for my evening meal. The more closely we approached the dugout the less I liked the prospect of reëntering it. One plan of escape had failed. I was sure the ruffians had no intention of permitting me to leave them and inform the stage people of their presence in the country.

One more plan suggested itself to me, and I lost no time in trying it. Dropping one of the sage-hens, I asked the man behind me to pick it up. As he was groping for it in the darkness, I pulled one of my Colt's revolvers, and hit him a terrific blow over the head. He dropped to the ground, senseless.

Wheeling about, I saw that the other man, hearing the fall, had turned, his hand upon his revolver. It was no time for argument. I fired and killed him. Then, leaping on my horse, I dug the spurs into his sides, and back down the trail we went, over the rocks and rough ground toward safety.

My peril was far from past. At the sound of the shot the six men in the dugout tumbled forth in hot haste. They stopped an instant at the scene of the shooting, possibly to revive the man I had stunned and to learn from him what had happened.

They were too wise to mount their horses, knowing that, afoot, they could make better time over the rocky country than I could on horseback. Steadily I heard them gaining, and soon made up my mind that if I was to evade them at all I must abandon my horse.

Jumping off, I gave him a smart slap with the butt of my revolver which sent him down the valley. I turned and began to scramble up the mountainside.

I had climbed hardly forty feet when I heard them pass, following the sound of my horse's feet. I dodged behind a tree as they went by, and when I heard them firing farther down the trail I worked my way up the mountainside.

It was twenty-five miles to Horseshoe Station, and very hard traveling the first part of the way. But I got to the station, just before daylight, weary and footsore, but exceedingly thankful.

Tired as I was, I woke up the men at the station and told them of my adventure. Slade himself led the party that set out to capture my former hosts, and I went along, though nearly beat out.

Twenty of us, after a brisk ride, reached the dugout at ten o'clock in the morning. But the thieves had gone. We found a newly made grave where they had buried the man I had to kill, and a trail leading southwest toward Denver. That was all. But my adventure at least resulted in clearing the country of horse-thieves. Once the gang had gone, no more depredations occurred for a long time.

After a year's absence from home I began to long to see my mother and sisters again. In June, 1861, I got a pass over the stage-line, and returned to Leavenworth. The first rumblings of the great struggle that was soon to be known as the Civil War were already reverberating throughout the North; Sumter had been fired upon in April of that year. Kansas, as every schoolboy knows, was previously the bloody scene of some of the earliest conflicts.

My mother's sympathies were strongly with the Union. She knew that war was bound to come, but so confident was she in the strength of the Federal Government that she devoutly believed that the struggle could not last longer than six months at the utmost.

Fort Leavenworth and the town of Leavenworth were still important outfitting posts for the soldiers in the West and

Southwest. The fort was strongly garrisoned by regular troops. Volunteers were undergoing training. Many of my boyhood friends were enlisting. I was eager to join them.

But I was still the breadwinner of the family, the sole support of my sisters and my invalid mother. Not because of this, but because of her love for me, my mother exacted from me a promise that I would not enlist for the war while she lived.

But during the summer of 1861 a purely local company, know as the Red- Legged Scouts, and commanded by Captain Bill Tuff, was organized. This I felt I could join without breaking my promise not to enlist for the war, and join it I did. The Red-Legged Scouts, while they coöperated with the regular army along the borders of Missouri, had for their specific duty the protection of Kansas against raiders like Quantrell, and such bandits as the James Boys, the Younger Brothers, and other desperadoes who conducted a guerrilla warfare against Union settlers.

We had plenty to do. The guerrillas were daring fellows and kept us busy. They robbed banks, raided villages, burned buildings, and looted and plundered wherever there was loot or plunder to be had.

But Tuff was the same kind of a fighting man as they, and working in a better cause. With his scouts he put the fear of the law into the hearts of the guerrillas, and they notably decreased their depredations in consequence.

Whenever and wherever we found that the scattered bands were getting together for a general raid we would at once notify the regulars at Fort Scott or Fort Leavenworth to be ready for them. Quantrell once managed to collect a thousand men in a hurry, and to raid and sack Lawrence before the troops could head them off. But when we got on their trail they were driven speedily back into Missouri.

In the meantime we took care that little mischief was done by the gangs headed by the James Boys and the Youngers, who operated in Quantrell's wake and in small bands.

In the spring of '63 I left the Red-Legged Scouts to serve the Federal Government as guide and scout with the Ninth Kansas Cavalry. The Kiowas and Comanches were giving trouble along the old Santa Fe trail and among the settlements of western Kansas. The Ninth Kansas were sent to tame them and to protect immigrants and settlers.

This was work that I well understood. We had a lively summer, for the Indians kept things stirring, but after a summer of hard fighting we made them understand that the Great White Chief was a power that the Indians had better not irritate. November, '63, I returned with the command to Leavenworth. I had money in my pockets, for my pay had been $150 a month, and I was able to lay in an abundant supply of provisions for my family.

On the twenty-third day of December my mother passed away. Her life had been an extremely hard one, but she had borne up bravely under poverty and privation, supplying with her own teaching the education that the frontier schools could not give her children, and by her Christian example setting them all on a straight road through life.

Border ruffians killed her husband, almost within sight of her home. She passed months in terror and distress and, until I became old enough to provide for her, often suffered from direst poverty. Yet she never complained for herself; her only thoughts being for her children and the sufferings that were visited upon them because of their necessary upbringing in a rough and wild country.

My sister Julia was now married to Al Goodman, a fine and capable young man, and I was free to follow the promptings of an adventurous nature and go where my companions were fighting. In January, 1864, the Seventh Kansas Volunteers came to Leavenworth from the South, where they had been fighting since the early years of the war. Among them I found many of my old friends and schoolmates. I was no longer under promise not to take part in the war and I enlisted as a private.

In March of that year the regiment was embarked on steamboats and sent to Memphis, Tennessee, where we joined the command of General A.J. Smith. General Smith was organizing an army to fight the illiterate but brilliant Confederate General Forrest, who was then making a great deal of trouble in southern Tennessee.

While we were mobilizing near Memphis, Colonel Herrick of our regiment recommended me to General Smith for membership in a picked corps to be used for duty as scouts, messengers, and dispatch carriers. Colonel Herrick recounted my history as a plainsman, which convinced the commander that I would be useful in this special line of duty.

When I reported to General Smith, he invited me into his tent and inquired minutely into my life as a scout.

"You ought to be able to render me valuable service," he said.

When I replied that I should be only too glad to do so, he got out a map of Tennessee, and on it showed me where he believed General Forrest's command to be located. His best information was that the Confederate commander was then in the neighborhood of Okolona, Mississippi, about two hundred miles south, of Memphis.

He instructed me to disguise myself as a Tennessee boy, to provide myself with a farm horse from the stock in the camp, and to try to locate Forrest's main command. Having accomplished this, I was to gather all the information possible concerning the enemy's strength in men and equipment and defenses, and to make my way back as speedily as possible.

General Smith expected to start south the following morning, and he showed me on the map the wagon road he planned to follow, so that I might know where to find him on my return. He told me before we parted that the mission on which he was sending me was exceedingly dangerous. "If you are captured," he said, "you will be shot as a spy."

To this I replied that my Indian scouting trips had been equally dangerous, as capture meant torture and death, yet I had always willingly undertaken them.

"Do you think you can find Forrest's army?" he said. "Well, if you can't find an army as big as that you're a mighty poor scout," he said grimly.

General Smith then turned me over to the man who was in charge of what was called "the refuge herd," from which I found a mount built on the lines of the average Tennessee farm horse. This man also provided me with a suit of farmer's clothing, for which I exchanged my new soldier uniform, and a bag of provisions. Leading me about a mile from camp, he left me with the warning:

"Look out, young fellow. You're taking a dangerous trip." Then we shook hands and I began my journey.

I had studied carefully the map General Smith had shown me, and had a fairly accurate idea of the direction I was supposed to take. Following a wagon road that led to the south, I made nearly sixty miles the first night. The mare I had chosen proved a good traveler.

When morning came I saw a big plantation, with the owner's and negroes' houses, just ahead of me. I was anxious to learn how my disguise was going to work, and therefore rode boldly up to the house of the overseer and asked if I could get rest and some sort of breakfast.

In response to his inquiries I said I was a Tennesseean and on my way to Holly Springs. I used my best imitation of the Southern dialect, which I can still use on occasion, and it was perfectly successful. I was given breakfast, my mare was fed, and I slept most of the day in a haystack, taking up my journey again immediately after dinner.

Thereafter I had confidence in my disguise, and, while making no effort to fall into conversation with people, I did not put myself out to evade anyone whom I met. None of those with whom I talked suspected me of being a Northern spy.

At the end of a few days I saw that I was near a large body of troops. It was in the morning after a hard day-and-night ride. Fearing to approach the outposts looking weary and fagged out, I rested for an hour, and then rode up and accosted one of them. To his challenge I said I was a country boy, and had come in to see the soldiers. My father and brother, I said, were fighting with Forrest, and I was almost persuaded to enlist myself.

My story satisfied the guard and I was passed. A little farther on I obtained permission to pasture my horse with a herd of animals belonging to the Confederates and, afoot, I proceeded to the camp of the soldiers. By acting the part of the rural Tennesseean, making little purchases from the negro food-stands, and staring open-mouthed at all the camp life, I picked up a great deal of information without once falling under suspicion.

The question now uppermost in my mind was how I was going to get away. Toward evening I returned to the pasture, saddled my mare and rode to the picket line where I had entered.

Here, to my dismay, I discovered that the outposts had been recently changed.

But I used the same story that had gained admission for me. In a sack tied to my saddle were the food supplies I had bought from the negroes during the day. These, I explained to the outposts, were intended as presents for my mother and sisters back on the farm. They examined the sack, and, finding nothing contraband in it, allowed me to pass.

I now made all possible speed northward, keeping out of sight of houses and of strangers. On the second day I passed several detachments of Forrest's troops, but my training as a scout enabled me to keep them from seeing me.

Though my mare had proven herself an animal of splendid endurance, I had to stop and rest her occasionally. At such times I kept closely hidden. It was on the second morning after leaving Forrest's command that I sighted the advance guard of Smith's army. They halted me when I rode up, and for a time I had more trouble with them than I had had with any of Forrest's men. I was not alarmed, however, and when the captain told me that he would have to send me to the rear, I surprised him by asking to see General Smith.

"Are you anxious to see a big, fighting general?" he asked in amazement.

"Yes," I said. "I hear that General Smith can whip Forrest, and I would like to see any man who can do that."

Without any promises I was sent to the rear, and presently I noticed General Smith, who, however, failed to recognize me.

I managed, however, to draw near to him and ask him if I might speak to him for a moment.

Believing me to be a Confederate prisoner, he assented, and when I had saluted I said:

"General, I am Billy Cody, the man you sent out to the Confederate lines."

"Report back to your charge," said the general to the officer who had me in custody. "I will take care of this man."

My commander was much pleased with my report, which proved to be extremely accurate and valuable. The disguise he had failed to penetrate did not deceive my comrades of the Ninth Kansas, and when I passed them they all called me by name and asked me where I had been. But my news was for my superior officers, and I did not need the warning Colonel Herrick gave me to keep my mouth shut while among the soldiers.

General Smith, to whom I later made a full detailed report, had spoken highly of my work to Colonel Herrick, who was gratified to know that his choice of a scout had been justified by results.

It was not long before the whole command knew of my return, but beyond the fact that I had been on a scouting expedition, and had brought back information much desired by the commander, they knew nothing of my journey. The next morning, still riding the same mare and still wearing my Tennessee clothes, I rode out with the entire command in the direction of Forrest's army.

Before I had traveled five miles I had been pointed out to the entire command, and cheers greeted me on every side. As soon as an opportunity offered I got word with the general and asked if he had any further special orders for me.

"Just keep around," he said; "I may need you later on."

"But I am a scout," I told him, "and the place for a scout is ahead of the army, getting information."

"Go ahead," he replied, "and if you see anything that I ought to know about come back and tell me."

Delighted to be a scout once more, I made my way forward. The general had given orders that I was to be allowed to pass in and out the lines at will, so that I was no longer hampered by the activities of my own friends. I had hardly got beyond the sound of the troops when I saw a beautiful plantation house, on the porch of which was a handsome old lady and her two attractive daughters.

They were greatly alarmed when I came up, and asked if I didn't know that the Yankee army would be along in a few minutes and that my life was in peril. All their own men folks, they said, were in hiding in the timber.

"Don't you sit here," begged the old lady, when I had seated myself on the porch to sip a glass of milk for which I had asked her. "The Yankee troops will go right through this house. They will break up the piano and every stick of furniture, and leave the place in ruins. You are sure to be killed or taken prisoner."

By this time the advance guard was coming up the road. General Smith passed as I was standing on the porch. I saw that he had noticed me, though he gave no sign of having done so. As more troops passed, men began leaving their companies and rushing toward the house. I walked out and ordered them away in the name of the general. They all knew who I was, and obeyed, much to the astonishment of the old lady and her daughter.

Turning to my hostess, I said:

"Madam, I can't keep them out of your chicken-house or your smoke-house or your storerooms, but I can keep them out of your home, and I will."

I remained on the porch till the entire command had passed. Nothing was molested. Much pleased, but still puzzled, the old lady was now convinced that I was no Tennessee lad, but a sure-enough Yankee, and one with a remarkable amount of influence. When I asked for a little something to eat in return for what I had done, the best there was in the house was spread before me.

My hostess urged me to eat as speedily as possible, and be on my way. Her men folks, she said, would soon return from the timber, and if they learned that I was a Yank would shoot me on the spot. As she was speaking the back door was pushed open and three men rushed in. The old lady leaped between them and mc.

"Don't shoot him!" she cried. "He has protected our property and our lives." But the men had no murderous intentions.

"Give him all he wants to eat," said the eldest, "and we will see that he gets back to the Yankee lines in safety. We saw him from the treetops turn away the Yanks as he stood on the porch."

While I finished my meal they put all manner of questions to me, being specially impressed that a boy so young could have kept a great army from foraging so richly stocked a plantation. I told them that I was a Union scout, and that I had saved their property on my own responsibility.

"I knew you would be back here," I said. "But I was sure you wouldn't shoot me when you learned what I had done."

"You bet your life we won't!" they said heartily.

After dinner I was stocked Tip with all the provisions I wanted, and given a fine bottle of peach brandy, the product of the plantation. Then the men of the place escorted me to the rear-guard of the command, which I lost no time in joining. When I overtook the general and presented him with the peach brandy, he said gruffly:

"I hear you kept all the men from foraging on that plantation back yonder."

"Yes, sir," I said. "An old lady and her two daughters were alone there. My mother had suffered from raids of hostile soldiers in Kansas. I tried to protect that old lady, as I would have liked another man to protect my mother in her distress. I am sorry if I have disobeyed your orders and I am ready for any punishment you wish to inflict on me."

"My boy," said the general, "you may be too good-hearted for a soldier, but you have done just what I would have done. My orders were to destroy all Southern property. But we will forget your violation, of them."

General Smith kept straight on toward Forrest's stronghold. Ten miles from the spot where the enemy was encamped, he wheeled to the left and headed for Tupedo, Mississippi, reaching there at dark. Forrest speedily discovered that Smith did not intend to attack him on his own ground. So he broke camp, and, coming up to the rear, continued a hot fire through the next afternoon.

Arriving near Tupedo, General Smith selected, as a battleground, the crest of a ridge commanding the position Forrest had taken up. Between the two armies lay a plantation of four or five thousand acres. The next morning Forrest dismounted some four thousand cavalry, and with cavalry and artillery on his left and right advanced upon our position.

Straight across the plantation they came, while Smith rode back and forth behind the long breastworks that protected his men, cautioning them to reserve their fire till it could be made to tell. All our men were fighting with single shotguns. The first shot, in a close action, had to count, or a second one might never be fired.

I had been detailed to follow Smith as he rode to and fro. With an eye to coming out of the battle with a whole skin I had picked out a number of trees, behind which I proposed to drop my horse when the fighting got to close quarters. This was the fashion I had always employed in Indian fighting. As the Confederates got within good range, the order "Fire!" rang out.

At that instant I wheeled my horse behind a big oak tree. Unhappily for me the general was looking directly at me as this maneuver was executed.

When we had driven back and defeated Forrest's men I was ordered to report at General Smith's tent.

"Young man," said the General, when I stood before him, "you were recommended to me as an Indian fighter. What were you doing behind that tree!"

"That is the way we have to fight Indians, sir," I said. "We get behind anything that offers protection." It was twelve years later that I convinced General Smith that my theory of Indian fighting was pretty correct.

After the consolidation of the regular army, following the war, Smith was sent to the Plains as Colonel of the Seventh Cavalry. This was afterward known as Custer's regiment, and we engaged in the battle of the Little Big Horn, in which that gallant commander was slain. Smith's cavalry command was moving southward on an expedition against the Kiowas and Comanches in the Canadian River country, when I joined it as a scout.

Dick Curtis, acting as guide for Smith, had been sent on ahead across the river, while the main command stopped to water their horses. Curtis's orders were to proceed straight ahead for five miles, where the troops would camp. He was followed immediately by the advance guard, Smith and his staff following on. We had proceeded about three miles when three or four hundred Indians attacked us, jumping out of gullies and ravines, where they had been securely hidden. General Smith at once ordered the orderlies to sound the recall and retreat, intending to fall back quickly on the main command.

He was standing close beside a deep ravine as he gave the order. Knowing that the plan he proposed meant the complete annihilation of our force, I pushed my horse close to him.

"General," I said, "order your men into the ravine, dismount, and let number fours hold horses. Then you will be able to stand off the Indians. If you try to retreat to the main command you and every man under you will be killed before you have retreated a mile."

He immediately saw the sense of my advice. Issuing orders to enter the ravine, he dismounted with his men behind the bank. There we stood off the Indians till the soldiers in the rear, hearing the shots, came charging to the rescue and drove the Indians away. The rapidity with which we got into the ravine, and the protection its banks afforded us, enabled us to get away without losing a man. Had the general's original plan been carried out none of us would have come away to tell the story. I was summoned to the general's tent that evening.

"That was a brilliant suggestion of yours, young man," he said. "This Indian fighting is a new business to me. I realize that if I had carried out my first order not a man of us would ever have reached the command alive."

I said: "General, do you remember the battle of Tupedo?"

"I do," he said, with his chest expanding a little. "I was in command at that battle." The whipping of Forrest had been a particularly difficult and unusual feat, and General Smith never failed to show his pride in the achievement whenever the battle of Tupedo was mentioned.

"Do you remember," I continued, "the young fellow you caught behind a tree, and sent for him afterward to ask him why he did so?"

"Is it possible you are the man who found Forrest's command!" he asked in amazement. "I had often wondered what became of you," he said, when I told him I was the same man. "What have you been doing since the war!"

I told him I had come West as a scout for General Sherman in 1865 and had been scouting ever since. He was highly delighted to see me again, and from that time forward, as long as he remained on the Plains, I resumed my old position as his chief scout.

After the battle of Tupedo, Smith's command was ordered to Memphis, and from there sent by boat up the Mississippi. We of the cavalry disembarked at Cape Jardo, Smith remaining behind with the infantry, which came on later. General Sterling Price, of the Confederate army, was at this time coming out of Arkansas into southern Missouri with a large army. His purpose was to invade Kansas.

Federal troops were not then plentiful in the West. Smith's army from Tennessee, Blunt's troops from Kansas, what few regulars there were in Missouri, and some detachments of Kansas volunteers were all being moved forward to head off Price. Being still a member of the Ninth Kansas Cavalry, I now found myself back in my old country—just ahead of Price's army, which had now reached the fertile northwestern Missouri.

In carrying dispatches from General McNeil to General Blunt or General Pleasanton I passed around and through Price's army many times. I always wore the disguise of a Confederate soldier, and always escaped detection. Price fought hard and successfully, gaining ground steadily, till at Westport, Missouri, and other battlefields near the Kansas line, the Federal troops checked his advance.

At the Little Blue, a stream that runs through what is now Kansas City, he was finally turned south, and took up a course through southern Kansas.

Near Mound City a scouting party of which I was a member surprised a small detachment of Price's army. Our advantage was such that they surrendered, and while we were rounding them up I heard one of them say that we Yanks had captured a bigger prize than we suspected. When he was asked what this prize consisted of, the soldier said:

"That big man over yonder is General Marmaduke of the Southern army."

I had heard much of Marmaduke and greatly admired his dash and ability as a fighting man. Going over to him, I asked if there was anything I could do to make him comfortable. He said that I could. He hadn't had a bite to eat, and he wanted some food and wanted it right away.

He was surrounding a good lunch I had in my saddle-bag, while I was ransacking the saddle-bag of a comrade for a bottle of whisky which I knew to be there.

When we turned our prisoners over to the main command I was put in charge of General Marmaduke and accompanied him as his custodian to Fort Leavenworth. The general and I became fast friends, and our friendship lasted long after the war. Years after he had finished his term as Governor of Missouri he visited me in London, where I was giving my Wild West Show.

He was talking with me in my tent one day when the Earl of Lonsdale and Lord Harrington rode up, dismounted, and came over to where we were sitting.

I presented Marmaduke to them as the governor of one of America's greatest States and a famous Confederate general. Lonsdale, approaching and extending his hand, smiled and said:

"Ah, Colonel Cody, another one of your Yankee friends, eh?"

Marmaduke, who had risen, scowled. But he held out his hand. "Look here," he said, "I am much pleased to meet you, sir, but I want you first to understand distinctly that I am no Yank."

When I left General Marmaduke at Leavenworth and returned to my command, Price was already in retreat. After driving him across the Arkansas River I returned with my troop to Springfield, Missouri. From there I went, under General McNeil, to Fort Smith and other places on the Arkansas border, where he had several lively skirmishes, and one big and serious engagement before the war was ended.

The spring of 1865 found us again in Springfield, where we remained about two months, recuperating and replenishing our stock. I now got a furlough of thirty days and went to St. Louis, where I invested part of a thousand dollars I had saved in fashionable clothes and in rooms at one of the best hotels. It was while there that I met a young lady of a Southern family, to whom I paid a great deal of attention, and from whom I finally extracted a promise that if I would come back to St. Louis at the end of the war she would marry me.

On my return to Springfield I found an expedition in process of fitting out for a scouting trip through New Mexico and into the Arkansas River country, to look after the Indians. With this party I took part in a number of Indian fights and helped to save a number of immigrant trains from destruction. On our return to Fort Leavenworth we found General Sanborn and a number of others of the former Union leaders who had come to the border to make peace with the Indians.

The various tribes that roamed the Plains had heard of the great war, and, believing that it had so exhausted the white man that he would fall an easy prey to Indian aggression, had begun to arm themselves and make ready for great conquests. They had obtained great stores of arms and ammunition.

During the last two years of the war they had been making repeated raids and inflicting vast damage on the settlers.

At the close of the war, when the volunteers were discharged, I was left free to return to my old calling. The regular army was in course of consolidation. Men who had been generals were compelled to serve as colonels and majors. The consolidated army's chief business was in the West, where the Indians formed a real menace, and to the West came the famous fighting men under whose command I was destined to spend many of the eventful years to come.

❐

# Chapter-3.

At the close of the war, General William Tecumseh Sherman was placed at the head of the Peace Commission which had been sent to the border to take counsel with the Indians. It had become necessary to put an end to the hostility of the red man immediately either by treaty or by force. His raids on the settlers could be endured no longer.

The purpose of the party which Sherman headed was to confer with the greatest of the hostile chiefs. Treaties were to be agreed upon if possible. If negotiations for peace failed, the council would at least act as a stay of hostilities. The army was rapidly reorganizing, and it would soon be possible to mobilize enough troops to put down the Indians in case they refused to come to terms peaceably.

The camp of the Kiowas and Comanches—the first Indians with whom Sherman meant to deal—was about three hundred miles southwest of Leavenworth, in the great buffalo range, and in the midst of the trackless Plains.

By ambulance and on horseback, with wagons to carry the supplies, the party set out for its first objective—Council Springs on the Arkansas River, about sixty miles beyond old Fort Zarrah.

I was chosen as one of the scouts or dispatch carriers to

accompany the party. The guide was Dick Curtis, a plainsman of wide experience among the Indians.

When we arrived at Fort Zarrah we found that no road lay beyond, and learned that there was no water on the way. It was determined, therefore, to make a start at two o'clock in the morning. Curtis said this would enable us to reach our destination, sixty-five miles further on, by two o'clock the next afternoon.

The outfit consisted of two ambulances and one Government wagon, which carried the tents and supplies. Each officer had a horse to ride if he chose. If he preferred to ride in the ambulance his orderly was on hand to lead his horse for him.

We traveled steadily till ten o'clock in the morning, through herds of buffalo whose numbers were past counting. I remember that General Sherman estimated that the number of buffalo on the Plains at that time must have been more than eleven million. It required all the energy of the soldiers and scouts to keep a road cleared through the herds so that the ambulance might pass.

We breakfasted during the morning stop and rested the horses. For the men there was plenty of water, which we had brought along in canteens and camp kettles. There was also a little for the animals, enough to keep them from suffering on the way.

Two o'clock found us still making our way through the buffalo herds, but with no Council Springs in sight. Curtis was on ahead, and one of the lieutenants, feeling a little nervous, rode up to another of the scouts.

"How far are we from the Springs?" he inquired.

"I don't know," said the guide uneasily. "I never was over here before, but if any one knows where the Springs are that young fellow over there does." He pointed to me.

"When will we get to the Springs?" asked the officer, turning in my direction. "Never—if we keep on going the way we are now," I said.

"Why don't you tell the General that?" he demanded.

I said that Curtis was the guide, not I; whereupon he dropped back alongside the ambulance in which Sherman was riding and reported what had happened.

The General instantly called a halt and sent for the scouts. When all of us, including Curtis, had gathered round him he got out of the ambulance, and, pulling out a map, directed Curtis to locate the Springs on it.

"There has never been a survey made of this country, General," said Curtis. "None of these maps are correct."

"I know that myself," said Sherman. "How far are we from the Springs?"

The guide hesitated. "I have never been there but once," he said, "and then I was with a big party of Indians who did the guiding." He added that on a perfectly flat country, dotted with buffalo, he could not positively locate our destination. Unless we were sighted and guided by Indians we would have to chance it.

Sherman swung round on the rest of us. "Do any of you know where the Springs are?" he asked, looking directly at me.

"Yes, sir," I said, "I do."

"How do you know, Billy?" asked Curtis.

"I used to come over here with Charley Bath, the Indian trader," I said. "Where are we now?" asked Sherman.

"About twelve miles from the Springs. They are due south." "Due south! And we are traveling due west!"

"Yes, sir," I replied, "but if Mr. Curtis had not turned in a few minutes I was going to tell you."

So for twelve miles I rode with Sherman, and we became fast friends. He asked me all manner of questions on the way, and I found that he knew my father well, and remembered his tragic death in Salt Creek Valley. He asked what had become of the rest of the family and all about my career. By the end of the ride I had told him my life history.

As we were riding along together, with the outfit following on, I noticed pony tracks from time to time, and knew that we were nearing the Springs. Presently I said:

"General, we are going to find Indians at the Springs when we reach there." "How do you know?"

"We have been riding where ponies have been grazing for the last mile." "I haven't seen any tracks," said the General in surprise. "Show me one."

I jumped off my horse, and, thrusting the buffalo grass aside, I pointed out many tracks of barefooted ponies. "When we rise that ridge," I told him, "we shall see the village, and thousands of ponies and Indian lodges."

In a very few minutes this prophecy came true. Curtis and the other scouts with the officers rode up quickly behind us, and we all had a fine view of this wonderful sight of the desert—a great Indian camp. As we stood gazing at the spectacle we observed great excitement in the village. Warriors by the dozens were leaping on their horses and riding toward us, till at least a thousand of them were in the "receiving line."

"It looks to me as if we had better fall into position," said Sherman.

"It is not necessary," I said. "They have given us the peace sign. They are coming toward us without arms."

So Sherman, with General Harney, General Sanborn, and the other officers rode slowly forward to meet the oncoming braves.

"This is where you need Curtis," I told the General as he advanced. "He is the best Kiowa and Comanche interpreter on the Plains and he knows every one of these Indians personally."

Curtis was accordingly summoned and made interpreter, while I was assigned to remain about the commander's tent and given charge of the scouts.

As the Indians drew near with signs of friendliness, Curtis introduced the chiefs, Satanta, Lone Wolf, Kicking Bird, and others to General Sherman as the head of the Peace Commission.

The Indians, having been notified in advance of the coming of the Commission, had already selected a special spring for our camp and had prepared a great feast in honor of the meeting. To this feast, which was spread in the center of the village, the Commissioners were conducted, while the scouts and the escort went into camp.

The Indians had erected a great canopy of tanned buffalo skins on tepee poles. Underneath were robes for seats for the General and his staff, and thither they were led with great ceremony. Near by was a great fire on which, buffalo, antelope, and other animals were roasting. Even coffee and sugar had been provided, and the feast was served with tin plates for the meat and tin cups for the coffee. Another tribute to the customs of the guests was a complete outfit of knives and forks. Napkins, however, appeared to be lacking.

Indian girls, dressed in elaborate costumes, served the repast, the elder women preparing the food. Looking on, it seemed to me to be the most beautiful sight I had ever seen—the grim old generals, who for the last four and a half years had been fighting a great war sitting serenely and contentedly down to meat and drink with the chiefs of a wild, and, till lately, a hostile race.

After all had eaten, the great chief, Satanta, loaded the big peace-pipe, whose bowl was hewn from red stone, with a beautifully carved stem eighteen inches long. The pipe was passed from mouth to mouth around the circle. After the smoke was ended Satanta raised his towering bulk above the banqueters. He drew his red blanket around his broad shoulders, leaving his naked right arm free, for without his right arm an Indian is deprived of his real powers of oratory. Making signs to illustrate his every sentence, he spoke:

"My great white brothers, I welcome you to my camp and to my people. You can rest in safety, without a thought of fear, because our hearts are now good to you—because we hope that the words you are going to speak to us will make us glad that you have come. We know that you have come a long way to see us. We feel that you are going to give us or send us presents which will gladden the hearts of all my people.

"I know that you must be very tired, and as I see that your tents are pitched it would make our hearts glad to walk over to your village with you, where you can rest and sleep well, and we hope that you will dream of the many good things are going to send us and tell us when you rested.

"I have sent to your tents the choicest of young buffalo, deer, and antelope, and if there is anything else in my camp which will make your hearts glad I will be pleased to send it to you. If any of your horses should stray away, my young men will bring them back to you."

As the old chief concluded, General Sherman, rising, shook his hand and said:

"My red brother, your beautiful and romantic reception has deeply touched the hearts of my friends and myself. We most heartily thank you for it. When we are rested, and after we have slept in your wild prairie city, we should like to hold a council with the chiefs and warriors congregated here."

When the officers returned to their own camp they agreed that the feast was very grand, that the Indian maidens who served it were very pretty in their gay costumes and beautiful moccasins. Most of them, however, had observed that the hands of the squaws who did the cooking looked as if they had not touched water for several months. It stuck in the memory of some of the guests that, in their efforts to clean the tinware, the squaws had left more soap in the corners than was necessary. The coffee had a strong flavor of soap.

"If we are going to have a banquet every day," said one officer, "I think I'll do my eating in our own camp."

General Sherman reminded him that this would be highly impolite to the hosts, and ordered them, as soldiers, to make the best of the entertainment and to line up for mess when the Indians made a feast.

At ten o'clock the next morning the first session of the great council was held. For three days the white chiefs and the red chiefs sat in a circle under the canopy, and many promises of friendship were made by the Indians.

When the council was concluded, General Sherman sent for me.

"Billy," he said, "I want you to send two good men to Fort Ellsworth with dispatches, where they can be forwarded to Fort Riley, the end of the telegraph line. After your men are rested they can return to Fort Zarrah and join us." When the two men were instructed by the General and were on their way, he took me into his tent.

"I want to go to Bent's Fort on the Arkansas River," he said, "then to Fort St. Barine, on the Platte, and then to Laramie; after that we will go to Cottonwood Springs, then to Fort Kearney and then to Leavenworth. Can you guide me on that trip?"

I told him that I could, and was made guide, chief of scouts, and master of transportation, acting with an army officer as quartermaster.

At Bent's Fort another council of two days was held with the Indians. The journey homeward was made without difficulty. At Leavenworth I took leave of one of the noblest and kindest-hearted men I have ever known. In bidding me good-by, General Sherman said:

"I don't think these councils we have held will amount to much. There was no sincerity in the Indians' promises. I will see that the promises we made to them are carried out to the letter, but when the grass grows in the spring they will be, as usual, on the warpath. As soon as the regular army is organized it will have to be sent out here on the border to quell fresh Indian uprisings, because these Indians will give us no peace till they are thoroughly thrashed."

The General thanked me for my services, and told me he was very lucky to find me. "It is not possible that I will be with the troops when they come," he said. "They will be commanded by General Philip Sheridan. You will like Sheridan. He is your kind of a man. I will tell him about you when I see him. I expect to hear great reports of you when you are guiding the United States army over the Plains, as you have so faithfully guided me. The quartermaster has instructions to pay you at the rate of $150 a month, and as a special reward I have ordered that you be paid $2000 extra. Good-by! I know you will have good luck, for you know your business."

After the departure of General Sherman I made a brief visit to my sisters in Salt Creek Valley, and for a time, there being no scouting work to do, drove stage between Plum Creek and Fort Kearney.

I was still corresponding with Miss Frederici, the girl I had left behind me in St. Louis. My future seemed now secure, so I decided that it was high time I married and settled down, if a scout can ever settle down. So, surrendering my stage job, I returned to Leavenworth and embarked for St. Louis by boat. After a week's visit at the home of my fiancée we were quietly married at her home. I made, I suppose, rather a wild-looking groom. My brown hair hung down over my shoulders, and I had just started a little mustache and goatee. I was dressed in the Western fashion, and my appearance was, to say the least, unusual. We were married at eleven o'clock in the morning, and took the steamer Morning Star at two in the afternoon for our honeymoon journey home.

As we left our carriages and entered the steamer, my wife's father and mother and a number of friends accompanying us, I noticed that I was attracting considerable excited attention. A number of people, men and women, were on the deck. As we passed I heard them whispering:

"There he is! That's him! I'd know him in the dark!"

It was very plain to me that these observations were not particularly friendly. The glares cast at me were openly hostile. While we were disposing our baggage in our stateroom—I had hired the bridal chamber—I heard some of my wife's friends asking her father if he knew who I was, and whether I had any credentials. He replied that he had left the matter of credentials to his daughter.

"Well," said one of the party, "these people on board are excursionists from Independence, and they say this son-in-law of yours is the most desperate outlaw, bandit, and house-burner on the frontier!"

The old gentleman was considerably disturbed at this report. He made up his mind to get a little first-hand information, and he took the most direct means of getting it.

"Who are you?" he asked, walking over to me. "The people on board don't give you a very good recommendation."

"Kindly remember," I replied, "that we have had a little war for the past five years on the border. These people were on one side and I on the other, and it is natural that they shouldn't think very highly of me."

My argument was not convincing. "I am going to take my daughter home again," said my father-in-law, and started toward the stateroom.

I besought him to leave the decision to her, and for the next ten minutes I pleaded my case with all the eloquence I could command. I was talking against odds, for my wife, as well as her parents' friends, were all ardent Southerners, and I am proud to say that after fifty years of married life, she is still as strongly "Secesh" as ever. But when I put the case to her she said gamely that she had taken me for better or for worse and intended to stick to me.

She was in tears when she said good-by to her parents and friends, and still in tears after they had left. I tried to comfort her with assurances that when we came among Northern people I would not be regarded as such a desperate character, but my consolation was of little avail. At dinner the hostile stares that were bent on me from our neighbors at table did not serve to reassure her. It was some comfort to me afterward when the captain sent for me and told me that he knew me, that my Uncle Elijah was his old-time friend, and one of the most extensive shippers on the steamboat line. "It is shameful the way these people are treating you," he said, "but let it pass, and when we get to Independence everything will be all right."

But everything was not all right. In the evening, when I led my wife out on the floor of the cabin, where the passengers were dancing, every dancer immediately walked off the floor, the men scowling and the women with their noses in the air. All that night my wife wept while I walked the floor.

At daybreak, when we stopped for wood, I heard shots and shouting. Walking out on deck, I saw the freed negroes who composed the crew scrambling back on board. The steamboat was backing out in the stream. Later I learned that my fellow passengers had wired up the river that I was on board, and an armed party had ridden down to "get" me.

I quickly returned to the stateroom, and, diving into my trunk, took out and buckled on a brace of revolvers which had done excellent service in times past. This action promptly confirmed my wife's suspicions. She was now certain that I was the bandit I had been accused of being. I had no time to reason with her now. Throwing my coat back, so that I rested my hands on the butts of my revolvers, I strolled out through the crowd.

One or two men who had been doing a great deal of loud talking a few minutes past backed away, as I walked past and looked them squarely in the eyes. Nothing more was said, and soon I reached the steward's office, unmolested. Here I found a number of men dressed in blue uniforms. They told me they were discharged members of the Eighth Indiana Volunteers. They were traveling to Kansas, steerage, saving their money so they might have it to invest in homes when they reached their destination. They had all heard of me, and now proposed to arm and defend me should there be any further hostile demonstrations. I gladly welcomed their support, more for my wife's sake than for my own.

"My wife," I said, "firmly believes that I am an outlaw."

"You can't blame her," said the spokesman of the party, "after what has happened. But wait till she gets among Union people and she will learn her mistake. We know your history, and of your recent services to General Sherman. We know that old 'Pap' Sherman wouldn't have an outlaw in his service. If you had seen some of the interviews he has given out about your wife's father and his friends there would have been trouble at the start."

My new-found friends did not do things by halves. In order to be able to give a ball in the cabin they exchanged their steerage tickets for first-class passage. That night the ball was given, with my wife and myself as the guests of honor.

The Independence crowd, observing the preparations for the ball, demanded that the captain stop at the first town and let them off. They saw that the tide had turned, and were apprehensive of reprisals. The captain told them that if they should behave like ladies and gentlemen all would be well.

That night they stood outside looking in while my wife, now quite reassured, was introduced to the ladies and gentlemen from Indiana, and danced till she was weary.

We looked for trouble when we reached Independence the next day. There was a bigger crowd than usual on the levee, but when it was seen that my Yankee friends had their Spencer carbines with them all was quiet. As we pulled out the old captain called me outside.

"Cody, it is all over now," he said. "But don't you think you were the only restless man on board. When I backed out into the river the other night I had to leave four of my best deckhands either dead or wounded on the bank. I will never forget the way you walked out through the crowd with that pair of guns in your hand. I have heard of the execution these weapons can do when they get in action."

When we stopped at Kansas City I telegraphed to Leavenworth that we were coming. As the boat approached the Leavenworth levee my soldier friends were out on deck in their dress uniforms, and I stood on the deck, my bride on my arm. Soon we heard the music of the Fort Leavenworth band and the town band, and crowds of citizens were on the wharf as the boat tied up.

The commandant of the fort, D.R. Anthony, the Mayor of Leavenworth, my sisters, and hundreds of my friends came rushing aboard the boat to greet us. That night we were given a big banquet to which my soldier chums and their wives were invited. My wife had a glorious time. After it was all over, she put her arms about my neck and cried:

"Willy, I don't believe you are an outlaw at all!"

I had reluctantly promised my wife that I would abandon the Plains. It was necessary to make a living, so I rented a hotel in Salt Creek Valley, the same hotel my mother had formerly conducted, and set up as a landlord.

It was a typical frontier hotel, patronized by people going to and from the Plains, and it took considerable tact and diplomacy to conduct it successfully. I called the place "The Golden-Rule House," and tried to conduct it on that principle. I seemed to have the qualifications necessary, but for a man who had lived my kind of life it proved a tame employment. I found myself sighing once more for the freedom of the Plains. Incidentally I felt sure I could make money as a plainsman, and, now that I had a wife to support, money had become a very important consideration.

I sold out the Golden-Rule House and set out alone for

Saline, Kansas, which was then at the end of construction of the Kansas Pacific Railway. On my way I stopped at Junction City, were I again met my old friend, Wild Bill, who was scouting for the Government, with headquarters at Fort Ellsworth, afterward called Fort Harker. He told me more scouts were needed at the Post, and I accompanied him to the fort, where I had no difficulty in securing employment.

During the winter of 1866-67 I scouted between Fort Ellsworth and Fort Fletcher. I was at Fort Fletcher in the spring of 1867 when General Custer came out to accompany General Hancock on an Indian expedition. I remained here till the post was flooded by a great rise of Big Creek, on which it was located. The water overflowed the fortifications, rendering the place unfit for further occupancy, and it was abandoned by the Government. The troops were removed to Fort Hays, a new post, located farther west, on the south fork of Big Creek. It was while I was at Fort Hays that I had my first ride with the dashing Custer. He had come up from Ellsworth with an escort of only ten men, and wanted a guide to pilot him to Fort Larned, sixty-five miles distant.

When Custer learned that I was at the Post he asked that I be assigned to duty with him. I reported to him at daylight the next day—none too early, as Custer, with his staff and orderlies, was already in the saddle. When I was introduced to Custer he glanced disapprovingly at the mule I was riding.

"I am glad to meet you, Cody," he said. "General Sherman has told me about you. But I am in a hurry, and I am sorry to see you riding that mule."

"General," I returned, "that is one of the best horses at the fort."

"It isn't a horse at all," he said, "but if it's the best you've got we shall have to start."

We rode side by side as we left the fort. My mule had a fast walk, which kept the general's horse most of the time in a half-trot.

His animal was a fine Kentucky thoroughbred, but for the kind of work at hand I had full confidence in my mount. Whenever Custer was not looking I slyly spurred the mule ahead, and when he would start forward I would rein him in and pat him by way of restraint, bidding him not to be too fractious, as we hadn't yet reached the sandhills. In this way I set a good lively pace— something like nine miles an hour—all morning.

At Smoky Hill River we rested our animals. Then the general, who was impatient to be off, ordered a fresh start. I told him we had still forty miles of sandhills to cross, and advised an easier gait.

"I have no time to waste on the road," he said. "I want to push right ahead."

Push right ahead we did. I continued quietly spurring my mule and then counseling the brute to take it easy. Presently I noticed that the escort was stringing out far behind, as their horses became winded with the hard pace through the sand. Custer, looking back, noticed the same thing.

"I think we are setting too fast a pace for them, Cody," he said, but when I replied that I thought this was merely the usual pace for my mule and that I supposed he was in a hurry he made no further comment.

Several times during the next forty miles we had to stop to wait for the escort to close up. Their horses, sweating and panting, had reached almost the limit of their endurance. I continued patting my animal and ordering him to quiet down, and Custer at length said:

"You seem to be putting it over me a little today."

When we reached a high ridge overlooking Pawnee Fork we again waited for our lagging escort. As we waited I said:

"If you want to send a dispatch to the officer in command at Fort Larned, I will be pleased to take it down for you. You can follow this ridge till you come to the creek and then follow the valley right down to the fort."

Custer swung around to the captain, who had just ridden up, and repeated to him my instructions as to how to reach the fort. "I shall ride ahead with Cody," he added. "Now, Cody, I am ready for you and that mouse-colored mule."

The pace I set for General Custer from that time forward was "some going." When we rode up to the quarters of Captain Daingerfield Parker, commandant of the post, General Custer dismounted, and his horse was led off to the stables by an orderly, while I went to the scouts' quarters. I was personally sure that my mule was well cared for, and he was fresh as a daisy the next morning.

After an early breakfast I groomed and saddled my mule, and, riding down to the general's quarters, waited for him to appear. I saluted as he came out, and said that if he had any further orders I was ready to carry them out.

"I am not feeling very pleasant this morning, Cody," he said. "My horse died during the night."

I said I was very sorry his animal got into too fast a class the day before.

"Well," he replied, "hereafter I will have nothing to say against a mule. We will meet again on the Plains. I shall try to have you detailed as my guide, and then we will have time to talk over that race."

A few days after my return to Fort Hays the Indians made a raid on the Kansas Pacific Railroad, killing five or six men and running off a hundred or more horses and mules. The news was brought to the commanding officer, who immediately ordered

Major Arms, of the Tenth Cavalry, to go in pursuit of the raiders. The Tenth Cavalry was a negro regiment. Arms took a company, with one mountain howitzer, and I was sent along as scout.

On the second day out we discovered a large party of Indians on the opposite side of the Saline River, and about a mile distant. The party was charging down on us and there was no time to lose. Arms placed his howitzer on a little knoll, limbered it up, and left twenty men to guard it. Then, with the rest of the command, he crossed the river to meet the redskins.

Just as he had got his men across the stream we heard a terrific shouting. Looking back toward the knoll where the gun had been left, we saw our negro gun-guard flying toward us, pursued by more than a hundred Indians. More Indians were dancing about the gun, although they had not the slightest notion what to do with it.

Arms turned back with his command and drove the redskins from their useless prize. The men dismounted and took up a position there.

A very lively fight followed. Five or six men, including Major Arms, were wounded, and a number of the horses were shot. As the fight proceeded, the enemy seemed to become steadily more numerous. It was apparent that reinforcements were arriving from some large party in the rear.

The negro troops, who had been boasting of what they would do to the Indians, were now singing a different tune.

"We'll jes' blow 'em off'm de fahm," they had said, before there was an enemy in sight. Now, every time the foe would charge us, some of the darkies would cry:

"Heah dey come! De whole country is alive wif 'em. Dere must be ten thousand ob dem. Massa Bill, does you-all reckon we is ebber gwine to get out o' heah?"

The major, who had been lying under the cannon since receiving his wound, asked me if I thought there was a chance to get back to the fort. I replied that there was, and orders were given for a retreat, the cannon being left behind.

During the movement a number of our men were killed by the deadly fire of the Indians. But night fell, and in the darkness we made fairly good headway, arriving at Fort Hays just at daybreak. During our absence cholera had broken out at the post. Five or six men were dying daily. For the men there was a choice of dangers—going out to fight the Indians on the prairie, or remaining in camp to be stricken with cholera. To most of us the former was decidedly the more inviting.

"The Rise and Fall of Modern Rome"—was the chapter of frontier history in which I next figured. For a time I was part owner of a town, and on my way to fortune. And then one of those quick changes that mark Western history in the making occurred and I was left—but I will tell you the story.

At the town of Ellsworth, which I visited one day while carrying dispatches to Fort Harker, I met William Rose, who had a contract for trading on the right-of-way of the Kansas Pacific near Fort Hays. His stock had been stolen by the Indians, and he had come to Ellsworth to buy more.

Rose was enthusiastic about a project for laying out a town site on the west side of Big Creek, a mile from the fort, where the railroad was to cross.

When, in response to a request for my opinion, I told him I thought the scheme a big one, he invited me to come in as a partner. He suggested that after the town was laid out and opened to the public we establish a store and saloon.

I thought it would be a grand thing to become half owner

of a town, and at once accepted the proposition. We hired a railroad engineer to survey the town site and stake it into lots. Also we ordered a big stock of the goods usually kept in a general merchandise store on the frontier. This done, we gave the town the ancient and historical name of Rome. As a starter we donated lots to anyone who would build on them, reserving for ourselves the corner lots and others which were best located. These reserved lots we valued at two hundred and fifty dollars each.

When the town was laid out I wrote my wife that I was worth $250,000, and told her I wanted her to get ready to come to Ellsworth by rail. She was then visiting her parents at St. Louis, with our baby daughter whom we had named Arta.

I was at Ellsworth to meet her when she arrived, bringing the baby. Besides three or four wagons, in which the supplies for the new general store and furniture for the little house I had built were loaded, I had a carriage for her and the baby. The new town of Rome was a hundred miles west. I knew that it would be a dangerous trip, as the Indians had long been troublesome along the railroad, and I realized the danger more fully because of the presence of my wife and little daughter.

A number of immigrants bound for the new town accompanied us.

The first night out I formed the men into a company, one squad to stand watch while the others slept. All the early part of the evening I went the rounds of the camp, much to my wife's annoyance.

"Why are you away so much?" she kept asking. "It is lonesome here, and I need you."

Rather than let her know of my uneasiness about the Indians, I told her I was trying to sell lots to the men while they were en route. As the night wore on and everything seemed quiet I prepared to get a little rest. I did not take my clothes off, and, much to my wife's surprise, slept with my rifle and revolvers close by me. I had just dropped off to sleep when I heard shots, and knew they could mean nothing but Indians.

The attacking party was small and we were fully prepared. When they discovered this they fired a few shots and galloped away.

The second night was almost a repetition of the first. After another party had been repulsed, Mrs. Cody asked me if I had brought her and the baby out on the Plains to be killed.

"This is the kind of a life I lead every day and get fat on it," I said. But she did not seem to think it especially congenial.

Everybody turned out to greet us when we arrived in Rome. Even the gambling-hall houses and the dance-halls closed in our honor. The next day we moved into our little house. That night there was a veritable fusillade of revolver shots outside the window.

"What is that?" asked Mrs. Cody. "Just a serenade," I said.

"Are yon firing blank cartridges?"

"No. If it became known that revolvers were loaded with blank cartridges around here we would soon lose some of our most valued citizens.

Everybody in town, from the police judge to dishwashers, carries a pistol." "Why?"

"To keep law and order."

That puzzled my wife. She said that in St. Louis policemen kept law and order, and wanted to know why we didn't have them to do it out here. I informed her that a policeman would not last very long in a town like this, which was perfectly true.

On my return from a hunting trip a few days later I met a man who had come into town on the stage-coach, and whom Mrs. Cody had seen looking over the town site from every possible angle. He told me he thought I had selected a good town site—and I agreed with him. He asked me to go for a ride around the surrounding country with him the next day. I told him I was going on a buffalo hunt. He had never killed a buffalo, he said. He wanted to get a fine head to take back with him, and would be grateful if I would take him with me. I promised to see that he got a nice head if he came along, and early the next morning rode down to his hotel. He was dressed in a smart hunting costume and had his rifle. We started for the plains, my wagons following to gather up the meat we should kill.

As we rode out I explained to him how I hunted. "I kill as many buffalo as I want," I said. "This I call a 'run.' The wagons come along afterward and the butchers cut the meat and load it." When I went out on my "run" I told him where to shoot to kill. But when my work was done I met him coming back crestfallen. He had failed to get his buffalo down, although he had shot him three times.

"Come along with me," I said. "I see another herd over there. I am going to change saddles with you and let you ride the best buffalo horse on the Plains."

He was astonished and delighted to think I would let him ride Brigham, the most famous buffalo horse in the West. When we drew near the herd I pointed out a fine four-year-old bull with a splendid head. I galloped alongside. Brigham spotted the buffalo I wanted, and after my companion's third shot the brute fell. My pupil was overjoyed with his success, and appeared to be so grateful to me that I felt sure I should be able to sell him three or four blocks of Rome real estate at least. I invited him to take dinner, and served as part of the repast the meat of the buffalo he had shot. The next morning he looked me up and told me he wanted to make a proposition to me.

"What is it?" I asked. I had thought I was the one who was going to make a proposition.

"I will give you one-eighth of this town site," he said.

The nerve of this proposal took me off my feet. Here was a total stranger offering me one-eighth of my own town site as a reward for what I had done for him.

I told him that if he killed another buffalo I would have to hog-hobble him and send him out of town; then rode off and left him.

This magnanimous offer occurred right in front of my own house. My wife overheard it, and also my reply.

As I rode away, he called out that he wanted to explain, but I was thoroughly disgusted.

"I have no time to listen to you," I shouted over my shoulder.

I was bound out on a buffalo hunt to get meat for the graders twenty miles away on the railroad, and I kept right on going. Three days afterward I rode back over the ridge above the town of Rome and looked down on it.

I took several more looks. The town was being torn down and carted away. The balloon-frame buildings were coming apart section by section. I could see at least a hundred teams and wagons carting lumber, furniture, and everything that made up the town over the prairies to the eastward.

My pupil at buffalo hunting was Dr. Webb, president of the town-site company of the Kansas Pacific. After I had ridden away without listening to his explanations he had invited the citizens of Rome to come over and see where the new railroad division town of Hays City was to be built. He supplied them with wagons for the journey from a number of rock wagons that had been lent him by the Government to assist him in the location of a new town. The distance was only a mile, and he got a crowd. At the town site of Hays City he made a speech, telling the people who he was and what he proposed to do. He said the railroad would build its repair-shops at the new town, and there would be employment for many men, and that Hays City was destined soon to be the most important place on the Plains. He had already put surveyors to work on the site. Lots, he said, were then on the market, and could be had far more reasonably than the lots in Rome.

My fellow-citizens straightway began to pick out their lots in the new town. Webb loaned them the six-mule Government wagons to bring over their goods and chattels, together with the timbers of their houses. When I galloped into Rome that day there was hardly a house left standing save my little home, our general store, and a few sod-houses and dugouts.

Mrs. Cody and the baby were sitting on a drygoods box when I rode up to the store. My partner, Rose, stood near by, whistling and whittling.

"My word, Rose! What has become of our town!" I cried. Rose could make no answer. Mrs. Cody said:

"You wrote me you were worth $250,000."

"We've got no time to talk about that now," I said. "What made this town move away?"

"You ought to have taken Mr. Webb's offer," was her answer.

"Who the dickens is Webb?" I stormed. Rose looked up from his whittling. "Bill," he said, "that little flapper-jack was the president of the town-site company for the K.P. Railroad, and he's run such a bluff on our citizens about a new town site that is going to be a division-point that they've all moved over there."

"Yes," commented Mrs. Cody, "and where is your $250,000?"

"Well, I've got to make it yet," I said, and then to Rose: "How did the fall hit you?"

"What fall?"

"From millionaire to pauper."

"It hasn't got through hitting me yet," he said solemnly.

Rose went back to his grading contract, and I resumed my work as a buffalo hunter. When the Perry House, the Rome hotel, was moved to Hays City and rebuilt there, I took my wife and daughter and installed them there.

It was hard to descend from the rank of millionaires to that of graders and buffalo hunters, but we had to do it. The rise and fall of modern Rome had made us, and it broke us!

❒

# Chapter-4.

I soon became better acquainted with Dr. Webb, through whose agency our town of Rome had fallen almost overnight. We visited him often in Hays, and eventually he presented my partner Rose and myself each with two lots in the new town.

Webb frequently accompanied me on buffalo-hunting excursions; and before he had been on the prairie a year there were few men who could kill more buffalo than he.

Once, when I was riding Brigham, and Webb was mounted on a splendid thoroughbred bay, we discovered a band of Indians about two miles distant, maneuvering so as to get between us and the town. A gallop of three miles brought us between them and home; but by that time they had come within three-quarters of a mile of us. We stopped to wave our hands at them, and fired a few shots at long range. But as there were thirteen in the party, and they were getting a little too close, we turned and struck out for Hays. They sent some scattering shots in pursuit, then wheeled and rode off toward the Saline River.

When there were no buffalo to hunt I tried the experiment of hitching Brigham to one of our railroad scrapers, but he was not gaited for that sort of work. I had about given up the idea of extending his usefulness to railroading when news came that buffaloes were coming over the hill. There had been none in the vicinity for some time. As a consequence, meat was scarce.

I took the harness from Brigham, mounted him bareback and started after the game, being armed with my new buffalo killer which I had named "Lucretia Borgia," an improved breech-loading needle-gun which I had obtained from the Government.

As I was riding toward the buffaloes I observed five men coming from the fort. They, too, had seen the herd and had come to join the chase. As I neared them I saw that they were officers, newly arrived at the fort, a captain and four lieutenants.

"Hello, my friend!" sang out the captain as they came up. "I see you are after the same game we are."

"Yes, sir," I returned. "I saw those buffaloes coming. We are out of fresh meat, so I thought I would get some."

The captain eyed my cheap-looking outfit closely. Brigham, though the best buffalo horse in the West, was decidedly unprepossessing in appearance.

"Do you expect to catch any buffaloes on that Gothic steed!" asked the captain, with a laugh.

"I hope so."

"You'll never catch them in the world, my fine fellow. It requires a fast horse to overtake those animals."

"Does it?" I asked innocently.

"Yes. But come along with us. We're going to kill them more for the sport than anything else. After we take the tongues and a piece of the tenderloin, you may have what is left."

Eleven animals were in the herd, which was about a mile distant. I noticed they were making toward the creek for water. I knew buffalo nature, and was aware that it would be difficult to turn them from their course. I therefore started toward the creek to head them off, while the officers dashed madly up behind them.

The herd came rushing up past me, not a hundred yards distant, while their pursuers followed, three hundred yards in the rear.

"Now," thought I, "is the time to get in my work." I pulled the blind bridle from Brigham, who knew as well as I did what was expected of him. The moment he was free of the bridle he set out at top speed, running in ahead of the officers. In a few jumps he brought me alongside the rear buffalo.

Raising old "Lucretia Borgia," I killed the animal with one shot. On went Brigham to the next buffalo, ten feet farther along, and another was disposed of. As fast as one animal would fall, Brigham would pass to the next, getting so close that I could almost touch it with my gun. In this fashion I killed eleven buffaloes with twelve shots.

As the last one dropped my horse stopped. I jumped to the ground. Turning round to the astonished officers, who had by this time caught up, I said:

"Now, gentlemen, allow me to present you with all the tongues and tenderloins from these animals that you want."

Captain Graham, who, I soon learned, was the senior officer, gasped. "Well, I never saw the like before! Who are you, anyway?"

"My name is Cody," I said.

Lieutenant Thompson, one of the party, who had met me at Fort Harker, cried out: "Why, that is Bill Cody, our old scout." He introduced me to his comrades, Captain Graham and Lieutenants Reed, Emmick, and Ezekial.

Graham, something of a horseman himself, greatly admired Brigham. "That horse of yours has running points," he admitted.

The officers were a little sore at not getting a single shot; but the way I had killed the buffaloes, they said, amply repaid them for their disappointment. It was the first time they had ever seen or heard of a white man running buffaloes without either saddle or bridle.

I told them Brigham knew nearly as much about the business as I did. He was a wonderful horse. If the buffalo did not fall at the first shot he would stop to give me a second chance; but if, on the second shot, I did not kill the game, he would go on impatiently as if to say: "I can't fool away my time by giving you more than two shots!"

Captain Graham told me that he would be stationed at Fort Hays during the summer. In the event of his being sent out on a scouting expedition he wanted me as scout and guide. I said that although I was very busy with my railroad contract I would be glad to go with him.

That night the Indians unexpectedly raided our horses, and ran off five or six of the best work-teams. At daylight I jumped on Brigham, rode to Fort Hays, and reported the raid to the commanding officer. Captain Graham and Lieutenant Emmick were ordered out with their company of one hundred colored troops. In an hour we were under way. The darkies had never been in an Indian fight and were anxious to "sweep de red debbils off de face ob de earth." Graham was a dashing officer, eager to make a record, and it was with difficulty that I could trail fast enough to keep out of the way of the impatient soldiers. Every few moments the captain would ride up to see if the trail was freshening, and to ask how soon we would overtake the marauders.

At the Saline River we found the Indians had stopped only to graze and water the animals and had pushed on toward Solomon. After crossing the river they made no effort to conceal their trail, thinking they were safe from pursuit. We reached Solomon at sunset. Requesting Captain Graham to keep his command where it was, I went ahead to try to locate the redmen.

Riding down a ravine that led to the river, I left my horse, and, creeping uphill, looked cautiously over the summit upon Solomon. In plain sight, not a mile away, was a herd of horses grazing, among them the animals which had been stolen from us. Presently I made out the Indian camp, noted its "lay," and calculated how best we could approach it.

Graham's eyes danced with excitement when I reported the prospect of an immediate encounter. We decided to wait until the moon rose, and then make a sudden dash, taking the redskins by surprise.

We thought we had everything cut and dried, but alas! just as we were nearing the point where we were to take the open ground and make our charge, one of the colored gentlemen became so excited that he fired his gun.

We began the charge immediately, but the warning had been sounded. The Indians at once sprang to their horses, and were away before we reached their camp. Captain Graham shouted, "Follow me, boys!" and follow him we did, but in the darkness the Indians made good their escape. The bugle sounded the recall, but some of the darkies did not get back to camp until the next morning, having, in their fright, allowed the horses to run wherever it suited them to go.

We followed the trail awhile the next day, but it became evident that it would be a long chase, and as we were short of rations we started back to camp. Captain Graham was bitterly disappointed at being cheated out of a fight that seemed at hand. He roundly cursed the darky who bad given, the warning with his gun. That gentleman, as a punishment, was compelled to walk all the way back to Fort Hays.

The western end of the Kansas Pacific was at this time in the heart of the buffalo country. Twelve hundred men were employed in the construction of the road. The Indians were very troublesome, and it was difficult to obtain fresh meat for the hands. The company therefore concluded to engage expert hunters to kill buffaloes.

Having heard of my experience and success as a buffalo hunter, Goddard Brothers, who had the contract for feeding the men, made me a good offer to become their hunter. They said they would require about twelve buffaloes a day—twenty-four hams and twelve humps, as only the hump and hindquarters of each animal were utilized. The work was dangerous.

Indians were riding all over that section of the country, and my duties would require me to journey from five to ten miles from the railroad every day in order to secure the game, accompanied by only one man with a light wagon to haul the meat back to camp. I demanded a large salary, which they could well afford to pay, as the meat itself would cost them nothing. Under the terms of the contract which I signed with them, I was to receive five hundred dollars a month, agreeing on my part to supply them with all the meat they wanted.

Leaving Rose to complete our grading contract, I at once began my career as a buffalo hunter for the Kansas Pacific. It was not long before I acquired a considerable reputation, and it was at this time that the title "Buffalo Bill" was conferred upon me by the railroad hands. Of this title, which has stuck to me through life, I have never been ashamed.

During my engagement as hunter for the company, which covered a period of eighteen months, I killed 4,280 buffaloes and had many exciting adventures with the Indians, including a number of hairbreadth escapes, some of which are well worth relating.

One day, in the spring of 1868, I mounted Brigham and started for Smoky Hill River. After a gallop of twenty miles I reached the top of a small hill overlooking that beautiful stream. Gazing out over the landscape, I saw a band of about thirty Indians some half-mile distant. I knew by the way they jumped on their horses they had seen me as soon as I saw them.

My one chance for my life was to run. I wheeled my horse and started for the railroad. Brigham struck out as if he comprehended that this was a life- or-death matter. On reaching the next ridge I looked around and saw the Indians, evidently well mounted, and coming for me full speed. Brigham put his whole strength into the flight, and for a few minutes did some of the prettiest running I ever saw. But the Indians had nearly as good mounts as he, and one of their horses in particular, a spotted animal, gained on me steadily.

Occasionally the brave who was riding this fleet horse would send a bullet whistling after me. Soon they began to strike too near for comfort. The other Indians were strung out along behind, and could do no immediate damage. But I saw that the fellow in the lead must be checked, or a stray bullet might hit me or the horse. Suddenly stopping Brigham, therefore, I raised old "Lucretia" to my shoulder and took deliberate aim, hoping to hit either the horse or the rider. He was not eighty yards behind me. At the crack of the rifle down went the horse. Not waiting to see if he regained his feet, Brigham and I went fairly flying toward our destination. We had urgent business just then and were in a hurry to attend to it.

The other Indians had gained while I stopped to drop the

leader. A volley of shots whizzed past me. Fortunately none of them hit. Now and then, to return the compliment, I wheeled and fired. One of my shots broke the leg of one of my pursuers' mounts.

But seven or eight Indians now remained in dangerous proximity to me. As their horses were beginning to lag, I checked Brigham to give him an opportunity to get a few extra breaths. I had determined that if the worst came to the worst I would drop into a buffalo wallow, where I might possibly stand off my pursuers. I was not compelled to do this, for Brigham carried me through nobly.

When we came within three miles of the railroad track, where two companies of soldiers were stationed, one of the outposts gave the alarm. In a few minutes, to my great delight, I saw men on foot and on horseback hurrying to the rescue. The Indians quickly turned and galloped away as fast as they had come. When I reached my friends, I turned Brigham over to them. He was led away and given the care and rub-down that he richly deserved.

Captain Nolan of the Tenth Cavalry now came up with forty men, and on hearing my account of what had happened determined to pursue the Indians. I was given a cavalry horse for a remount and we were off.

Our horses were all fresh and excellent stock. We soon began shortening the distance between ourselves and the fugitives. Before they had fled five miles we overtook them and killed eight of their number. The others succeeded in making their escape. Upon coming to the place where I had dropped the spotted horse that carried the leader of my pursuers I found that my bullet had struck him in the forehead, killing him instantly. He was a fine animal, and should have been engaged in better business.

On our return we found old Brigham grazing contentedly. He looked up inquiring, as if to ask if we had punished the redskins who pursued us. I think he read the answer in my eyes.

Another adventure which deserves a place in these reminiscences occurred near the Saline River. My companion at the time was Scotty, the butcher who accompanied me on my hunts, to cut up the meat and load it on the wagon for hauling to the railroad camp.

I had killed fifteen buffaloes, and we were on our way home with a wagonload of meat when we were jumped by a big band of Indians.

I was mounted on a splendid horse belonging to the company, and could easily have made my escape, but Scotty had only the mule team, which drew the wagon as a means of flight, and of course I could not leave him.

To think was to act in those days. Scotty and I had often talked of what we would do in case of a sudden attack, and we forthwith proceeded to carry out the plan we had made.

Jumping to the ground, we unhitched the mules more quickly than that operation had ever been performed before. The mules and my horse we tied to the wagon. We threw the buffalo hams on the ground and piled them about the wheels so as to form a breastwork. Then, with an extra box of ammunition and three or four extra revolvers which we always carried with us, we crept under the wagon, prepared to give our visitors a reception they would remember.

On came the Indians, pell-mell, but when they got within a hundred yards of us we opened such a sudden and galling fire that they held up and began circling about us.

Several times they charged. Their shots killed the two mules and my horse. But we gave it to them right and left, and had the satisfaction of seeing three of them fall to the ground not more than fifty feet away.

When we had been cooped up in our little fort for about an hour we saw the cavalry coming toward us, full gallop, over the prairie. The Indians saw the soldiers almost as soon as we did. Mounting their horses, they disappeared down the cañon of the creek. When the cavalry arrived we had the satisfaction of showing them five Indians who would be "good" for all time. Two hours later we reached the camp with our meat, which we found to be all right, although it had a few bullets and arrows imbedded in it.

It was while I was hunting for the railroad that I became acquainted with Kit Carson, one of the most noted of the guides, scouts, and hunters that the West ever produced. He was going through our country on his way to Washington. I met him again on his return, and he was my guest for a few days in Hays City. He then proceeded to Fort Lyon, Colorado, near which his son-in-law, Mr. Boggs, resided. His health had been failing for some time, and shortly afterward he died at Mr. Boggs's residence on Picket Wire Creek.

Soon after the adventure with Scotty I had my celebrated buffalo shooting contest with Billy Comstock, a well-known guide, scout, and interpreter.

Comstock, who was chief of scouts at Fort Wallace, had a reputation of being a successful buffalo hunter, and his friends at the fort—the officers in particular—were anxious to back him against me.

It was arranged that I should shoot a match with him, and the preliminaries were easily and satisfactorily arranged. We were to hunt one day of eight hours, beginning at eight o'clock in the morning. The wager was five hundred dollars a side, and the man who should kill the greater number of buffaloes from horseback was to be declared the winner. Incidentally my title of "Buffalo Bill" was at stake.

The hunt took place twenty miles east of Sheridan. It had been well advertised, and there was a big "gallery." An excursion party, whose members came chiefly from St. Louis and numbered nearly a hundred ladies and gentlemen, came on a special train to view the sport. Among them was my wife and my little daughter Arta, who had come to visit me for a time.

Buffaloes were plentiful. It had been agreed that we should go into the herd at the same time and make our "runs," each man killing as many animals as possible. A referee followed each of us, horseback, and counted the buffaloes killed by each man. The excursionists and other spectators rode out to the hunting-grounds in wagons and on horseback, keeping well out of sight of the buffaloes, so as not to frighten them until the time came for us to dash into the herd. They were permitted to approach closely enough to see what was going on.

For the first "run" we were fortunate in getting good ground. Comstock was mounted on his favorite horse. I rode old Brigham. I felt confident that I had the advantage in two things: first, I had the best buffalo horse in the country; second, I was using what was known at the time as a needle-gun, a breech-loading Springfield rifle, caliber .50. This was "Lucretia," the weapon of which I have already told you. Comstock's Henry rifle, though it could fire more rapidly than mine, did not, I felt certain, carry powder and lead enough to equal my weapon in execution.

When the time came to go into the herd, Comstock and I dashed forward, followed by the referees. The animals separated. Comstock took the left bunch, I the right. My great forte in killing buffaloes was to get them circling by riding my horse at the head of the herd and shooting their leaders. Thus the brutes behind were crowded to the left, so that they were soon going round and round.

This particular morning the animals were very accommodating. I soon had them running in a beautiful circle. I dropped them thick and fast till I had killed thirty-eight, which finished my "run."

Comstock began shooting at the rear of the buffaloes he was chasing, and they kept on in a straight line. He succeeded in killing twenty-three, but they were scattered over a distance of three miles. The animals I had shot lay close together.

Our St. Louis friends set out champagne when the result of the first run was announced. It proved a good drink on a Kansas prairie, and a buffalo hunter proved an excellent man to dispose of it.

While we were resting we espied another herd approaching. It was a small drove, but we prepared to make it serve our purpose. The buffaloes were cows and calves, quicker in their movements than the bulls. We charged in among them, and I got eighteen to Comstock's fourteen.

Again the spectators approached, and once more the champagne went round. After a luncheon we resumed the hunt. Three miles distant we saw another herd. I was so far ahead of my competitor now that I thought I could afford to give an exhibition of my skill. Leaving my saddle and bridle behind, I rode, with my competitor, to windward of the buffaloes.

I soon had thirteen down, the last one of which I had driven close to the wagons, where the ladies were watching the contest. It frightened some of the tender creatures to see a buffalo coming at full speed directly toward them, but I dropped him in his tracks before he had got within fifty yards of the wagon. This finished my "run" with a score of sixty-nine buffaloes for the day. Comstock had killed forty-six.

It was now late in the afternoon. Comstock and his backers gave up the idea of beating me. The referee declared me the winner of the match, and the champion buffalo hunter of the Plains.

On our return to camp we brought with us the best bits of meat, as well as the biggest and best buffalo heads. The heads I always turned over to the company, which found a very good use for them. They were mounted in the finest possible manner and sent to the principal cities along the road, as well as to the railroad centers of the country. Here they were prominently placed at the leading hotels and in the stations, where they made an excellent advertisement for the road Today they attract the attention of travelers almost everywhere. Often, while touring the country, I see one of them, and feel reasonably certain that I brought down the animal it once ornamented. Many a wild and exciting hunt is thus called to my mind.

In May, 1868, the Kansas Pacific track was pushed as far as Sheridan. Construction was abandoned for the time, and my services as buffalo hunter were no longer required. A general Indian war was now raging all along the Western borders. General Sheridan had taken up headquarters at Fort Hays, in order to be on the job in person. Scouts and guides were once more in great demand, and I decided to go back to my old calling.

I did not wish to kill my faithful old Brigham by the rigors of a scouting campaign. I had no suitable place to leave him, and determined to dispose of him. At the suggestion of a number of friends, all of whom wanted him, I put him up at a raffle, selling ten chances at thirty dollars each, which were all quickly taken. Ike

Bonham, who won him, took him to Wyandotte, Kansas, where he soon added fresh laurels to his already shining wreath. In the crowning event of a tournament he easily outdistanced all entries in a four-mile race to Wyandotte, winning $250 for his owner, who had been laughed at for entering such an unprepossessing animal.

I lost track of him after that. For several years I did not know what had become of him. But many years after, while in Memphis, I met Mr. Wilcox, who had once been superintendent of construction on the Kansas Pacific. He informed me that he owned Brigham, and I rode out to his place to take a look at my gallant old friend. He seemed to remember me, as I put my arms about his neck and caressed him like a long-lost child.

When I had received my appointment as guide and scout I was ordered to report to the commandant of Fort Larned, Captain Daingerfield Parker. I knew that it would be necessary to take my family, who had been with me at Sheridan, to Leavenworth and leave them there. This I did at once.

When I arrived at Larned, I found the scouts under command of Dick Curtis, an old-time scout of whom I have spoken in these reminiscences. Three hundred lodges of Kiowa and Comanche Indians were encamped near the fort. These savages had not yet gone on the warpath, but they were restless and discontented. Their leading chief and other warriors were becoming sullen and insolent. The Post was garrisoned by only two companies of infantry and one troop of cavalry. General Hazen, who was at the post, was endeavoring to pacify the Indians; I was appointed as his special scout.

Early one morning in August I accompanied him to Fort Zarrah, from which post he proceeded, without an escort, to Fort Harker. Instructions were left that the escort with me should return to Larned the next day. After he had gone I went to the sergeant in command of the squad and informed him I intended to return that afternoon. I saddled my mule and set out. All went well till I got about halfway between the two posts, when at Pawnee Rock I was suddenly jumped by at least forty Indians, who came rushing up, extending their hands and saying, "How?" "How?" These redskins had been hanging about Fort Larned that morning. I saw that they had on their warpaint, and looked for trouble.

As they seemed desirous to shake hands, however, I obeyed my first friendly impulse, and held out my hand. One of them seized it with a tight grip and jerked me violently forward. Another grabbed my mule by the bridle. In a few minutes I was completely surrounded.

Before I could do anything at all in my defense, they had taken my revolvers from the holsters and I received a blow on the head from a tomahawk which rendered me nearly senseless. My gun, which was lying across the saddle, was snatched from its place. Finally two Indians, laying hold of the bridle, started off in the direction of the Arkansas River, leading the mule, which was lashed by the other Indians who followed along after.

The whole crowd was whooping, singing, and yelling as only Indians can. Looking toward the opposite side of the river, I saw the people of a big village moving along the bank, and made up my mind that the redmen had left the Post, and were on the warpath in dead earnest.

My captors crossed the stream with me, and as we waded through the shallow water they lashed both the mule and me. Soon they brought me before an important-looking body of Indians, who proved to be the chiefs and principal warriors.

Among them I recognized, old Satanta and others whom I knew. I supposed that all was over with me.

All at once Satanta asked me where I had been, and I suddenly had an inspiration.

I said I had been after a herd of cattle or "Whoa-haws" as they called them. The Indians had been out of meat for several weeks, and a large herd of cattle which had been promised them had not arrived.

As soon as I said I had been after "Whoa-haws" old Satanta began questioning me closely. When he asked where the cattle were I replied that they were only a few miles distant and that I had been sent by General Hazen to inform him that the herd was coming, and that they were intended for his people. This seemed to please the old rascal. He asked if there were any soldiers with the herd. I said there were. Thereupon the chiefs held a consultation. Presently Satanta asked me if the general had really said they were to have the cattle. I assured him that he had. I followed this by a dignified inquiry as to why his young men had treated me so roughly.

He intimated that this was only a boyish freak, for which he was very sorry. The young men had merely wanted to test my courage. The whole thing, he said, was a joke. The old liar was now beating me at the lying game, but I did not care, since I was getting the best of it.

I did not let him suspect that I doubted his word. He ordered the young men to restore my arms and reprimanded them for their conduct. He was playing a crafty game, for he preferred to get the meat without fighting if possible, and my story that soldiers were coming had given him food for reflection.

After another council the old man asked me if I would go

and bring the cattle down. "Of course," I told him. "Such are my instructions from General Hazen."

In response to an inquiry if I wanted any of his young men to accompany me I said that it would be best to go alone. Wheeling my mule around, I was soon across the river, leaving the chief firmly believing that I was really going for the cattle, which existed only in my imagination.

I knew if I could get the river between me and the Indians I would have a good three-quarters of a mile start of them and could make a run for Fort Larned. But as I reached the river bank I looked about and saw ten or fifteen Indians who had begun to suspect that all was not as it should be.

The moment my mule secured a good foothold on the bank I urged him into a gentle lope toward the place where, according to my story, the cattle were to be brought.

Upon reaching the top of the ridge and riding down the other side out of view, I turned my mount and headed westward for Fort Larned. I let him out for all he was worth, and when I reached a little rise and looked back the Indian village lay in plain sight.

My pursuers were by this time on the ridge I had passed over, and were looking for me in every direction. Soon they discovered me, and discovered also that I was running away. They struck out in swift pursuit. In a few minutes it became painfully evident that they were gaining.

When I crossed Pawnee Fork, two miles from the Post, two or three of them were but a quarter of a mile behind. As I gained the opposite side of the creek I was overjoyed to see some soldiers in a Government wagon a short distance away. I yelled at the top of my lungs that the Indians were after me.

When Denver Jim, an old scout, who was with the party, was

informed that there were ten or fifteen Indians in the pursuit he said:

"Let's lay for them."

The wagon was driven hurriedly in among the trees and low box-elder bushes, and secreted, while we waited. We did not wait long. Soon up came the Indians, lashing their horses, which were blowing and panting. We let two of them pass, then opened a lively fire on the next three or four, killing two at the first volley. The others discovering that they had run into an ambush, whirled around and ran back in the direction from which they had come. The two who had passed heard the firing and made their escape.

The Indians that were killed were scalped, and we appropriated their arms and equipment. Then, after catching the horses, we made our way into the Post. The soldiers had heard us firing, and as we entered the fort drums were beating and the buglers were sounding the call to fall in. The officers had thought Satanta and his warriors were coming in to capture the fort.

That very morning, two hours after General Hazen had left, the old chief drove into the Post in an ambulance which he had received some months before from the Government. He seemed angry and bent on mischief. In an interview with Captain Parker, the ranking officer, he asked why General Hazen had left the fort without supplying him with beef cattle. The captain said the cattle were then on the road, but could not explain why they were delayed.

The chief made numerous threats. He said that if he wanted to he could capture the whole Post. Captain Parker, who was a brave man, gave him to understand that he was reckoning beyond his powers. Satanta finally left in anger. Going to the sutler's store, he sold his ambulance to the post-trader, and a part of the proceeds he secretly invested in whisky, which could always be secured by the Indians from rascally men about a Post, notwithstanding the military and civil laws.

He then mounted his horse and rode rapidly to his village. He returned in an hour with seven or eight hundred of his warriors, and it looked as if he intended to carry out his threat of capturing the fort. The garrison at once turned out. The redskins, when within a half mile, began circling around the fort, firing several shots into it.

While this circling movement was taking place, the soldiers observed that the whole village had packed up and was on the move. The mounted warriors remained behind some little time, to give their families an opportunity to get away. At last they circled the Post several times more, fired a few parting shots, and then galloped over the prairie to overtake the fast-departing village. On their way they surprised and killed a party of woodchoppers on Pawnee Fork, as well as a party of herders guarding beef cattle.

The soldiers with the wagon I had opportunely met at the crossing had been out looking for the bodies of these victims, seven or eight in all. Under the circumstances it was not surprising that the report of our guns should have persuaded the garrison that Satanta's men were coming back to make their threatened assault.

There was much excitement at the Post. The guards had been doubled. Captain Parker had all the scouts at his headquarters. He was seeking to get one of them to take dispatches to General Sheridan at Fort Hays. I reported to him at once, telling him of my encounter and my escape.

"You were lucky to think of that cattle story, Cody," he said. "But for that little game your scalp would now be ornamenting a Kiowa lodge."

"Cody," put in Dick Curtis, "the captain is trying to get somebody to take dispatches to General Sheridan. None of the scouts here seem willing to undertake the trip. They say they are not well enough acquainted with the country to find the way at night."

A storm was coming up, and it was sure to be a dark night. Not only did the scouts fear they would lose the way, but, with hostile Indians all about, the undertaking was exceedingly dangerous. A large party of redskins was known to be encamped at Walnut Creek, on the direct road to Fort Hays.

Observing that Curtis was obviously trying to induce me to volunteer, I made an evasive answer. I was wearied from my long day's ride, and the beating I received from the Indians had not rested me any. But Curtis was persistent. He said:

"I wish you were not so tired, Bill. You know the country better than the rest of us. I'm certain you could go through."

"As far as the ride is concerned," I said, "that would not matter. But this is risky business just now, with the country full of hostile Indians. Still, if no other man will volunteer I will chance it, provided I am supplied with a good horse. I am tired of dodging Indians on a Government mule."

At this, Captain Nolan, who had been listening, said:

"Bill, you can have the best horse in my company."

I picked the horse ridden by Captain Nolan's first sergeant. To the captain's inquiry as to whether I was sure I could find my way, I replied:

"I have hunted on every acre of ground between here and Fort Hays. I can almost keep my route by the bones of the dead buffaloes."

"Never fear about Cody, captain," Curtis added; "he is as good in the dark as he is in the daylight."

By ten o'clock that night I was on my way to Fort Hays, sixty-five miles distant across the country.

It was pitch-dark, but this I liked, as it lessened the probability of the Indians' seeing me unless I stumbled on them by accident. My greatest danger was that my horse might run into a hole and fall, and in this way get away from me. To avoid any such accident I tied one end of my rawhide lariat to my belt and the other to the bridle. I did not propose to be left alone, on foot, on that prairie.

Before I had traveled three miles the horse, sure enough, stepped into a prairie dog's hole. Down he went, throwing me over his head. He sprang to his feet before I could catch the bridle, and galloped away into the darkness. But when he reached the end of his lariat he discovered that he was picketed to Bison William. I brought him up standing, recovered my gun, which had fallen to the ground, and was soon in the saddle again.

Twenty-five miles from Fort Larned the country became rougher, and I had to travel more carefully. Also I proceeded as quietly as possible, for I knew I was in the vicinity of the Indians who had been lately encamped on Walnut Creek. But when I came up near the creek I unexpectedly rode in among a herd of horses. The animals became frightened, and ran off in all directions. Without pausing to make any apology, I backed out as quickly as possible.

But just at that minute a dog, not fifty yards away, set up a howl. Soon I heard Indians talking. They had been guarding the horses, and had heard the hoofbeats of my horse. In an instant they were on their ponies and after me.

I urged my mount to full speed up the creek bottom, taking chances of his falling into a hole. The Indians followed me as fast as they could, but I soon outdistanced them.

I struck the old Santa Fe trail ten miles from Fort Hays just at daybreak. Shortly after reveille I rode into the post, where Colonel Moore, to whom I reported, asked for the dispatches from Captain Parker for General Sheridan. He asked me to give them into his hands, but I said I preferred to hand them to the general in person. Sheridan, who was sleeping in the same building, heard our voices and bade me come into his room.

"Hello, Cody!" he said. "Is that you?"

"Yes, sir," I said. "I have dispatches for you."

He read them hurriedly, told me they were very important, and asked all about the outbreak of the Kiowas and Comanches. I gave him all the information I possessed.

"Bill," said General Sheridan, "you've had a pretty lively ride. I suppose you're tired after your long journey."

"Not very," I said.

"Come in and have breakfast with me."

"No, thank you. Hays City is only a mile from here. I know every one there and want to go over and have a time."

"Very well, do as you please, but come back this afternoon, for I want to see you."

I got little rest at Hays City, and yet I was soon to set out on another hard ninety-five-mile journey.

❒

# Chapter–5.

When I rode back to General Sheridan's headquarters, after a visit with old friends at Hays City, I noticed several scouts in a little group engaged in conversation on some important topic. Upon inquiry I learned that General Sheridan wanted a dispatch sent to Fort Dodge, a distance of ninety-five miles.

The Indians had recently killed two or three men engaged in carrying dispatches over this route. On this account none of the scouts were at all anxious to volunteer. A reward of several hundred dollars had failed to secure any takers.

The scouts had heard of what I had done the day before. They asked me if I did not think the journey to Fort Dodge dangerous. I gave as my opinion that a man might possibly go through without seeing an Indian, but that the chances were ten to one that he would have an exceedingly lively run before he reached his destination, provided he got there at all.

Leaving the scouts arguing as to whether any of them would undertake the venture, I reported to General Sheridan. He informed me that he was looking for a man to carry dispatches to Fort Dodge, and, while we were talking, Dick Parr, his chief of scouts, came in to inform him that none of his scouts would volunteer. Upon hearing this, I said:

"General, if no one is ready to volunteer, I'll carry your dispatches myself."

"I had not thought of asking you to do this, Cody," said the general. "You are already pretty hard-worked. But it is really important that these dispatches should go through."

"If you don't get a courier before four this afternoon, I'll be ready for business," I told him. "All I want is a fresh horse. Meanwhile I'll get a little more rest."

It was not much of a rest, however, that I got. I went over to Hays City and had a "time" with the boys. Coming back to the Post at the appointed hour, I found that no scout had volunteered. I reported to the general, who had secured an excellent horse for me. Handing me the dispatches, he said:

"You can start as soon as you wish. The sooner the better. And good luck to you, my boy!"

An hour later I was on my way. At dusk I crossed the Smoky Hill River. I did not urge my horse much, as I was saving him for the latter end of the journey, or for any run I might have to make should the "wild boys" jump me.

Though I kept a sharp watch through the night I saw no Indians, and had no adventures worth relating. Just at daylight I found myself approaching Saw Log River, having ridden about seventy-five miles.

A company of colored cavalry, under command of Major Cox, was stationed at this point. I approached the camp cautiously. The darky soldiers had a habit of shooting first and crying "Halt!" afterward. When I got within hearing distance I called out, and was answered by one of the pickets. I shouted to him not to shoot, informing him that I carried dispatches from Fort Hays. Then, calling the sergeant of the guard, I went up to the vidette, who at once recognized me, and took me to the tent of Major Cox.

This officer supplied me with a fresh horse, as requested by General Sheridan in a letter I brought to him. After an hour's sleep and a meal, I jumped into the saddle, and before sunrise was on my way. I reached Fort Dodge, twenty-five miles further on, between nine and ten o'clock without having seen a single Indian.

When I had delivered my dispatches, Johnny Austin, an old friend, who was chief of scouts at the Post, invited me to come to his house for a nap. When I awoke Austin told me there had been Indians all around the Post. He was very much surprised that I had seen none of them. They had run off cattle and horses, and occasionally killed a man. Indians, he said, were also very thick on the Arkansas River between Fort Dodge and Fort Larned, and had made considerable trouble. The commanding officer of Fort Dodge was very anxious to send dispatches to Fort Larned, but the scouts, like those at Fort Hays, were backward about volunteering. Fort Larned was my Post, and I wanted to go there anyhow. So I told Austin I would carry the dispatches, and if any of the boys wanted to go along I would be glad of their company. This offer was reported to the commanding officer. He sent for me, and said he would be glad to have me take the dispatches, if I could stand the trip after what I had already done.

"All I want is a fresh horse, sir," said I.

"I am sorry we haven't a decent horse," he replied, "but we have a reliable and honest Government mule, if that will do you."

"Trot out the mule," I told him. "It is good enough for me. I am ready at any time."

The mule was forthcoming. At dark I pulled out for Fort Larned, and proceeded without interruption to Coon Creek, thirty miles from Fort Dodge. I had left the wagon road some distance to the south, and traveled parallel to it. This I decided would be the safer course, as the Indians might be lying in watch for dispatch-bearers and scouts along the main road.

At Coon Creek I dismounted and led the mule down to the river to get a drink of water. While I was drinking the brute jerked loose and struck out down the creek. I followed him, trusting that he would catch his foot in the bridle rein and stop, but he made straight for the wagon road, where I feared Indians would be lurking, without a pause. At last he struck the road, but instead of turning back toward Fort Dodge he headed for Fort Larned, keeping up a jogtrot that was just too fast to permit me to overtake him.

I had my gun in hand, and was sorely tempted to shoot him more than once, and probably would have done so but for the fear of bringing the Indians down on me. But he was going my way, so I trudged along after him mile after mile, indulging from time to time in strong language regarding the entire mule fraternity. The mule stuck to the road and kept on for Fort Larned, and I did the same thing. The distance was thirty-five miles. As day was beginning to break, we—the mule and myself—found ourselves on a hill looking down on the Pawnee Fork, on which Fort Larned was located, only four miles away. When the sunrise gun sounded we were within half a mile of the Post.

I was thoroughly out of patience by this time.

"Now, Mr. Mule," I said, "it is my turn," and threw my gun to my shoulder. Like the majority of Government mules, he was not easy to kill. He died hard, but he died.

Hearing the report of the gun, the troops came rushing out to see what was the matter. When they heard my story they agreed that the mule had got no more than his deserts. I took the saddle and bridle and proceeded to the Post, where I delivered my dispatches to Captain Parker. I then went to Dick Curtis's house at the scouts' headquarters and put in several hours of solid sleep.

During the day General Hazen returned from Fort Harker. He had important dispatches to send to General Sheridan. I was feeling highly elated over my ride, and as I was breaking the scout records I volunteered for this mission.

The general accepted my offer, though he said there was no necessity of my killing myself. I said I had business which called me to Fort Hays, anyway, and that it would make no difference to the other scouts if he gave me the job, as none of them were particularly eager for the journey.

Accordingly, that night, I mounted an excellent horse, and next morning at daylight reached General Sheridan's headquarters at Fort Hays.

The general was surprised to see me, and still more so when I told him of the time I had made on the rides I had successfully undertaken. I believe this record of mine has never been beaten in a country infested with Indians and subject to blizzards and other violent weather conditions.

To sum up, I had ridden from Fort Larned to Fort Zarrah, a distance of sixty- five miles and back in twelve hours. Ten miles must be added to this for the distance the Indians took me across the Arkansas River. In the succeeding twenty-four hours I had gone from Fort Larned to Fort Hays, sixty-five miles, in eight hours. During the next twenty-four hours I rode from Fort Hays to Fort Dodge, ninety-five miles. The following night I traveled from Fort Dodge to Fort Larned, thirty miles on mule back and thirty-five miles on foot, in twelve hours, and the next night sixty-five miles more from Fort Larned to Fort Hays.

Altogether I had ridden and walked three hundred and sixty-five miles in fifty-eight hours, an average of over six miles an hour.

Taking into consideration the fact that most of this riding was done in the night over wild country, with no roads to follow, and that I had continually to look out for Indians, it was regarded at the time as a big ride as well as a dangerous one.

What I have set down here concerning it can be verified by referring to the autobiography of General Sheridan.

General Sheridan complimented me highly on this achievement. He told me I need not report back to General Hazen, as he had more important work for me to do. The Fifth Cavalry, one of the finest regiments of the army, was on its way to the Department of the Missouri, and he was going to send an expedition against the Dog Soldier Indians who were infesting the Republican River region.

"Cody," he said, "I am going to appoint you guide and chief of scouts of the command. How does that suit you?"

I told him it suited me first rate and thanked him for the honor.

The Dog Soldier Indians were a band of Cheyennes and of unruly, turbulent members of other tribes who would not enter into any treaty, and would have kept no treaty if they had made one. They had always refused to go on a reservation. They got their name from the word "Cheyenne," which is derived from chien, the French word for "dog."

On the third of October the Fifth Cavalry arrived at Fort Hays, and I at once began making the acquaintance of the members of the regiment. General Sheridan introduced me to Colonel Royal, the commander, whom I found a gallant officer and an agreeable gentleman. I also became acquainted with Major W.H. Brown, Major Walker, Captain Sweetman, Quartermaster E.M. Hays, and many others of the men with whom I was soon to be associated.

General Sheridan, being anxious to punish the Indians who had lately fought General Forsythe, did not give the regiment much of a rest. On October 5th it began the march to Beaver Creek country.

The first night we camped on the south fork of Big Creek, four miles west of Hays City. By this time I had become well acquainted with Major Brown and Captain Sweetman. They invited me to mess with them, and a jolly mess we had. There were other scouts with the command besides myself. I particularly remember Tom Kenahan, Hank Fields, and a character called "Nosey."

The morning of the 6th we pulled out to the north. During the day I was particularly struck with the appearance of the regiment. It was a beautiful command, and when strung out on the prairies with, a train of seventy-five six-mule wagons, ambulances, and pack-mules, I felt very proud of my position as guide and chief of scouts with such a warlike expedition.

Just as we were going into camp on the Saline River that night we ran into a band of some fifteen Indians. They saw us, and dashed across the creek, followed by some bullets which we sent after them.

This little band proved to be only a scouting party, so we followed it only a mile or two. Our attention was directed shortly to a herd of buffaloes, and we killed ten or fifteen for the command.

Next day we marched thirty miles. When we went into camp Colonel Royal asked me to go out and kill some buffaloes for the boys.

"All right, colonel," I said; "send along a wagon to bring in the meat."

"I am not in the habit of sending out my wagons till I know there is something to be hauled in," he said. "Kill your buffaloes first, and I'll send the wagons."

Without further words I went out on my hunt. After a short absence I returned and asked the colonel to send his wagons for the half-dozen buffaloes I had killed.

The following afternoon he again requested me to go out after buffaloes. I didn't ask for any wagons this time, but rode out some distance, and, coming upon a small herd, headed seven or eight of them directly for the camp. Instead of shooting them I ran them at full speed right into the place and then killed them one after another in rapid succession.

Colonel Royal, who witnessed the whole proceeding, was annoyed and puzzled, as he could see no good reason why I had not killed the buffaloes on the prairie.

Coming up angry, he demanded an explanation.

"I can't allow any such business as this, Cody," he exclaimed. "What do you mean by it!"

"I didn't care about asking for wagons this time, Colonel," I replied. "I thought I would make the buffaloes furnish their own transportation."

The colonel saw the force of my defense, and had no more to say on the subject.

No Indians had been seen in the vicinity during the day. Colonel Royal, having posted his pickets, supposed that everything was serene for the night. But before morning we were aroused by shots, and immediately afterward one of the mounted pickets came galloping into camp with the announcement that there were Indians close at hand. All the companies fell into line, prepared and eager for action. The men were still new to Indian fighting. Many of them were excited.

But, despite the alarm, no Indians made their appearance. Upon going to the post where the picket said he had seen them, none were to be found, nor could the faintest trace be discovered.

The sentinel, an Irishman, insisted that there certainly had been redskins there.

"But you must be mistaken," said the colonel.

"Upon me sowl, I'm not. As sure as me name's Pat Maloney, wan iv them red devils hit me on th' head with a club, so he did," persisted the picket.

When morning came we made a successful effort to clear up the mystery. Elk tracks were found in the vicinity, and it was undoubtedly a herd of elk that had frightened the picket. When he turned to flee he must have hit his head on an overhanging limb, which he supposed was the club of a redskin, bent on his murder. It was hard, however, to convince him that he could have been mistaken.

Three days' march brought us to Beaver Creek, where we encamped and where scouts were sent out in different directions. None of these parties discovered Indians, and they all returned to camp at about the same time. They found it in a state of excitement. A few hours before the return of the scouts the camp had been attacked by a party of redskins, who had killed two men and made off with sixty horses belonging to Company H.

That evening the command started on the trail of the horse thieves. Major Brown with two companies and three days' rations pushed ahead in advance of the main command. On the eighteenth day out, being unsuccessful in the chase, and nearly out of rations, the entire command marched toward the nearest railroad station and camped on the Saline river, three miles distant from Buffalo Tank.

While waiting for supplies we were joined by a new commanding officer, Brevet-Major-Greneral E.A. Carr, who was the senior major of the regiment and ranked Colonel Royal. He brought with him the celebrated Forsythe Scouts, who were commanded by Lieutenant Pepoon, a regular-army officer.

While in this camp, Major Brown welcomed a new lieutenant, who had come to fill a vacancy in the command. This was A.B. Bache, and on the day he was to arrive Major Brown had his private ambulance brought out and invited me to ride with him to the railroad station to meet the lieutenant. On the way to the depot he said:

"Now, Cody, we'll give Bache a lively little ride, and shake him up a little."

The new arrival was given a back seat in the ambulance when he got off the train, and we headed for the camp.

Presently Major Brown took the reins from his driver and at once began whipping the mules. When he had got them into a lively gallop he pulled out his revolver and fired several shots. The road was terribly rough and the night was intensely dark. We could not see where we were going, and it was a wonderful piece of luck that the wagon did not tip over and break our necks.

Finally Bache asked, good-humoredly:

"Is this the way you break in all your new lieutenants, Major?"

"Oh, no," returned the major. "But this is the way we often ride in this country. Keep your seat, Mr. Bache, and we'll take you through on time," he quoted, from Hank Monk's famous admonition to Horace Greeley.

We were now rattling down a steep hill at full speed. Just as we reached the bottom, the front wheels struck a deep ditch over which the mules had jumped. We were all brought up standing, and Bache plunged forward headlong to the front of the vehicle.

"Take the back seat, lieutenant," said Major Brown sternly.

Bache replied that he had been trying to do so, keeping his nerve and his temper. We soon got the wagon out of the ditch and resumed our drive. We swung into camp under full headway, and created considerable amusement. Everyone recognized the ambulance, and knew that Major Brown and I were out for a lark, so little was said about the exploit.

Next morning at an early hour the command started out on another Indian hunt. General Carr, who had a pretty good idea where he would be likely to find them, directed me to guide him by the nearest route to Elephant Fork, on Beaver Creek.

When we arrived at the South Fork of the Beaver, after two days' march, we discovered a fresh Indian trail. We had followed it hurriedly for eight miles when we discovered, on a bluff ahead, a large number of Indians.

General Carr ordered Lieutenant Pepoon's scouts and Company M to the front. Company M was commanded by Lieutenant Schinosky, a reckless dare-devil born in France, who was eager for a brush with the Indians.

In his anxiety to get into the fight he pushed his company nearly a mile in advance of the main command, when he was jumped by some four hundred Indians. Until our main force could come to his support he had as lively a little fight as any one could have asked for.

As the battle proceeded, the Indians continued to increase in numbers. At last it became apparent that we were fighting eight hundred or a thousand of them. The engagement was general. There were killed and wounded on both sides. The Indians were obviously fighting to give their families and village a chance to get away. We had surprised them with a larger force than they knew was in that part of the country. The battle continued steadily until dark. We drove them before us, but they fought stubbornly. At night they annoyed us by firing down into our camp from the encircling hills.

Several times it was necessary to order out the command to dislodge them and to drive them back where they could do no damage.

After one of these sallies, Captain Sweetman, Lieutenant Bache, and myself were taking supper together when "Whang!" came a bullet into Mr. Bache's plate. We finished our supper without having any more such close calls.

At daylight next morning we took the trail again, soon reaching the spot where the Indians had camped the night before. Here there had been a large village, consisting of five hundred lodges. Continuing our pursuit, we came in sight of the retreating village at two in the afternoon. At once the warriors turned back and gave us battle.

To delay us as much as possible they set fire to the prairie grass in front and on all sides of us. For the remainder of the afternoon we kept up a running fight. Repeatedly the Indians attempted to lead us away from the trail of their fleeing village. But their trail was easily followed by the tepee poles, camp-kettles, robes, and all the paraphernalia which proved too heavy to carry for long, and which were dropped in the flight. It was useless to try to follow them after nightfall, and at dark we went into camp.

Next morning we were again on the trail, which led north and back toward Beaver Creek. The trail crossed this stream a few miles from where we had first discovered the Indians. They had made almost a complete circle in the hope of misleading us.

Late in the afternoon we again saw them going over a hill far ahead. Toward evening the main body of warriors once more came back and fought us, but we continued to drive them till dusk, when we encamped for the night.

Soon the Indians, finding they could not hold out against us, scattered in every direction. We followed the main trail to the Republican River, where we made a cut-off and proceeded north toward the Platte.

Here we found that the Indians, traveling day and night, had got a long start. General Carr decided we had pushed them so hard and given them such a thorough scaring that they would leave the Republican country and go north across the railroad. It seemed, therefore, unnecessary to pursue them any further. Most of the Indians did cross the river near Ogallah as he predicted, and thence continued northward.

That night we returned to the Republican River and camped in a grove of cottonwoods, which I named Carr's Grove in honor of our commander.

General Carr informed me that the next day's march would be toward the headwaters of the Beaver. I said that the distance was about twenty-five miles, and he said we would make it the next day. Getting an early start in the morning, we struck out across the prairie. My position, as guide, was the advance guard. About two o'clock General Carr overtook me and asked me how far I supposed it was to water. I replied that I thought it was about eight miles, although we could see no sign of a stream ahead.

"Pepoon's scouts say you are traveling in the wrong direction," said the general. "They say, the way you are bearing, it will be fifteen miles before we strike any branches of the Beaver, and that when you do you will find no water, for they are dry at this season of the year in this locality."

"I think the scouts are mistaken, General," I said. "The Beaver has more water near its head than it has below. At the place where we will strike the stream we will find immense beaver dams, big and strong enough to cross your whole command if you wish."

"Well, go ahead," he said. "I leave it to you. But, remember, I don't want a dry camp."

"No danger of that," I returned and rode on. As I predicted, we found water seven or eight miles further on. Hidden in the hills was a beautiful little tributary of the Beaver. We had no trouble in selecting a fine camp with good spring water and excellent grass. Learning that the stream, which was but eight miles long, was without a name, the general took out his map, and, locating it, christened it Cody's Creek, which name it still bears.

Early the next morning we pulled out for the Beaver. As we were approaching the stream I rode on ahead of the advance guard in order to find a crossing. Just as I turned a bend of the creek "Bang!" went a shot, and down went my horse, accompanied by myself.

I disentangled myself and jumped clear of the carcass, turning my guns loose at two Indians whom I discovered in the direction from which the shot had come. In the suddenness of it all I missed my aim. The Indians fired two or three more shots, and I returned the compliment by wounding one of their horses.

On the other side of the creek I saw a few lodges moving rapidly away, and also mounted warriors. They also saw me and began blazing away with their guns. The Indians who had killed my horse were retreating across the creek, using a beaver dam for a bridge. I accelerated their pace by sending a few shots after them and also fired at the warriors across the stream. I was undecided as to whether it would be best to run back to the command on foot or to retain my position. The troops, I knew, would come up in a few minutes. The sound of the firing would hasten their arrival.

The Indians soon saw that I was alone. They turned and charged down the hill, and were about to cross the creek and corral me when the advance guard of the command appeared over the ridge and dashed forward to my rescue. Then the redskins whirled and made off.

When General Carr arrived he ordered Company I to pursue the band. I accompanied Lieutenant Brady, who commanded the company. For several hours we had a running fight with the Indians, capturing several of their horses and most of their lodges. At night we returned to the command, which by this time had crossed the dam.

For several days we scouted along the river. We had two or three lively skirmishes, but at last our supplies began to run low, and the general ordered us to return to Fort Wallace, which we reached three days afterward.

While the regiment remained here, waiting for orders, I spent most of my time hunting buffaloes. One day while I was out with a small party, fifty Indians jumped us, and we had a terrific battle for an hour. We finally managed to drive them off, with four of their warriors killed. With me were a number of excellent marksmen, and they did fine work, sending bullets thick and fast where they would do the most execution.

Two or three of our horses were hit. One man was wounded. We were ready and willing to stay with the Indians as long as they would stay with us. But they gave it up at last. We finished our hunt and returned to the Post with plenty of buffalo meat. Here we received the compliments of General Carr on our little fight.

In a few days orders came from General Sheridan to make

a winter campaign in the Canadian River country. We were to proceed to Fort Lyon on the Arkansas River and fit out for the expedition. Leaving Fort Wallace in November, 1868, we arrived at Fort Lyon in the latter part of the month, and began the work of outfitting.

Three weeks before this, General Penrose had left the Post with a command of three hundred men. He had taken no wagons with him. His supply train was composed of pack mules. General Carr was ordered to follow with supplies on Penrose's trail and to overtake him as soon as possible. I was particularly anxious to catch up with Penrose's command, as my old friend, "Wild Bill," was among his scouts.

For the first three days we followed the trail easily. Then we were caught in Freeze-Out Cañon by a fearful snowstorm. This compelled us to go into camp for a day.

It now became impossible longer to follow Penrose's trail. The ground was covered with snow, and he had left no sign to show in which direction he was going.

General Carr sent for me, and told me it was highly important that we should not lose the trail. He instructed me to take some scouts, and, while the command remained in camp, to push on as far as possible to seek for some sign that would indicate the direction Penrose had taken.

Accompanied by four men, I started out in a blinding snowstorm. We rode twenty-four miles in a southerly direction till we reached a tributary of the Cimarron. From here we scouted up and down the stream for a few miles, and at last turned up one of Penrose's old camps.

It was now late in the afternoon. If the camp was to come up the next day it was necessary for us to return immediately with our information.

We built a fire in a sheltered spot, broiled some venison we had shot during the day, and after a substantial meal I started back alone, leaving the others behind.

It was eleven o'clock when I got back into camp. A light was still burning in General Carr's tent. He was sitting up to await my return. He was overjoyed at the news I brought him. He had been extremely anxious concerning the safety of Penrose. Rousing up his cook, he ordered a hot supper for me, which, after my long, cold ride, I greatly appreciated. I passed the night in the general's tent, and woke the next morning fully refreshed and ready for a big day's work.

The snow had drifted deeply overnight, and the command had a hard tramp through it when it set out next morning for the Cimarron. In many ravines the drifts had filled in to a great depth. Often the teamsters had to shovel their way through.

At sundown we reached the Cimarron, and went into a nice warm camp. The next morning, on looking around, we found that Penrose, who was not encumbered with wagons, had kept on the west side of the Cimarron. Here the country was so rough that we could not stay on the trail with wagons.

But we knew that he would continue down the river, and the general gave orders to take the best route down-stream, which I found to be on the east side. Before we could make any headway with our wagon trains we had to leave the river and get out on the divide.

For some distance we found a good road, but suddenly we were brought up standing on a high table-land overlooking the beautiful winding creek that lay far below us. How to get the wagons down became a serious problem for the officers.

We were in the foothills of the rough Raton Mountains. The bluff we were on was steep and rugged.

"Cody," said General Carr, "we're in a nice fix now." "That's nothing," I replied.

"But you never can take the train down."

"Never mind the train, General. You are looking for a good camp. How does that valley suit you?"

"That will do," he said. "I can easily descend with the cavalry, but how to get the wagons down is a puzzler."

"By the time your camp is located the wagons will be there," I said.

"All right," he returned. "I'll leave it to you, inasmuch as you seem to want to be the boss." He ordered the command to dismount and lead the horses down the mountain. When the wagon-train, which was a mile in the rear, came up, one of the drivers asked:

"How are we going to get down there?"

"Run down, slide down, fall down—any way to get down," I told him.

"We never can do it," said another wagon-master. "It's too steep. The wagons will run over the mules."

"Oh, no," I said. "The mules will have to keep out of the way."

I instructed Wilson, the chief wagon-master, to bring up his mess-wagon. He drove the wagon to the brink of the bluff. Following my directions, he brought out extra chains with which we locked both wheels on each side, and then rough-locked them.

This done, we started the wagons down the hill. The wheel-horses, or rather the wheel-mules, were good on the hold back, and we got along beautifully till the wagon had nearly reached the bottom of the declivity. Then the wagon crowded the mules so hard that they started on the run and came galloping down into the valley to the spot General Carr had selected for his camp. There was not the slightest accident.

Three other wagons followed in the same way. In half an hour every wagon was in the camp. It was an exciting sight to see the six-mule teams come almost straight down the mountainside and finally break into a run. At times it seemed certain that the wagon must turn a somersault and land on the mules, but nothing of the kind happened.

Our march proved be a lucky one so far as gaining on Penrose was concerned. The route he had taken on the west side of the stream was rough and bad, and with our great wagon-train we made as many miles in one day as he had in seven.

His command had taken a high table-land whose sides were so steep that not even a pack mule could make the descent, and he had been obliged to retrace the trail for a great distance, losing three days while doing so.

The incident of this particular camp we had selected was an exciting turkey hunt. We found the trees along the river bank literally alive with turkeys.

After unsaddling the horses, two or three hundred soldiers surrounded a grove of timber, and there was a grand turkey round-up. Guns, clubs, and even stones were used as weapons. Of course, after the hunt we had roast turkey, boiled turkey, fried turkey, and turkey on toast for our fare, and in honor of the birds which had provided this treat we named the place Camp Turkey.

When we left camp we had an easy trail for several days. Penrose had taken a southerly direction toward the Canadian River. No Indians were to be seen, nor did we find any signs of them.

One day, while riding in advance of the command down San Francisco Creek, I heard some one calling my name from a little bunch of willow brush on the opposite bank of the stream. Looking closely at the spot, I saw a colored soldier.

"Sakes alive, Massa Bill, am dat you?" shouted the man, whom I recognized as a member of the Tenth Cavalry.

"Come out o' heah," I heard him call to someone behind him. "Heah's Massa Buffalo Bill." Then he sang out to me: "Massa Bill, is you got any hahdtack?"

"Nary a bit of hardtack, but the wagons will be along presently, and you can get all you want."

"Dat's de best news Ah's heahd fo' sixteen long days, Massa Bill." "Where's your command? Where's General Penrose?" I demanded. "Dunno," said the darky. "We got lost, an' we's been starvin' ever since."

By this time two other negroes had emerged from their hiding-place. They had deserted Penrose's command, which was out of rations and in a starving condition. They were trying to make their way back to old Fort Lyon. General Carr concluded, from what they could tell him, that Penrose was somewhere on Polladora Creek. But nothing definite was to be gleaned from the starving darkies, for they knew very little themselves.

General Carr was deeply distressed to learn that Penrose and his men were in such bad shape. He ordered Major Brown to start out the next morning with two companies of cavalry and fifty pack mules, loaded with provisions, and to make all possible speed to reach and relieve the suffering soldiers. I went with this detachment. On the third day out we found the half-famished soldiers encamped on the Polladora. The camp presented a pitiful sight. For over two weeks the men had only quarter rations and were now nearly starved to death. Over two hundred mules were lying dead, having succumbed to fatigue and starvation.

Penrose, having no hope that he would be found, had sent back a company of the Seventh Cavalry to Fort Lyon for supplies. As yet no word had been heard from them. The rations brought by Major Brown arrived none too soon. They were the means of saving many lives.

Almost the first man I saw after reaching the camp was my true and tried friend, "Wild Bill." That night we had a jolly reunion around the campfires.

When General Carr came up with his force, he took command of all the troops, as he was the senior officer. When a good camp had been selected he unloaded his wagons and sent them back to Fort Lyon for supplies. He then picked out five hundred of the best men and horses, and, taking his pack-train with him, started south for the Canadian River. The remainder of the troops were left at the supply camp.

I was ordered to accompany the expedition bound for the Canadian River. We struck the south fork of this stream at a point a few miles above the old adobe walls that were once a fort. Here Kit Carson had had a big Indian fight.

We were now within twelve miles of a new supply depot called Fort Evans, established for the Third Cavalry and Evans's expedition from New Mexico.

The scouts who brought this information reported also that they expected the arrival of a bull-train from New Mexico with a large quantity of beer for the soldiers.

"Wild Bill" and I determined to "lay" for this beer. That very evening it came along, and the beer destined for the soldiers at Fort Evans never reached them. It went straight down the thirsty throats of General Carr's command.

The Mexicans living near Fort Evans had brewed the beer.

They were taking it to Fort Evans to sell to the troops. But it found a better market without going so far. It was sold to our boys in pint cups, and, as the weather was very cold, we warmed it by putting the ends of our picket pins, heated red- hot, into the brew before we partook of it. The result was one of the biggest beer jollifications it has ever been my misfortune to attend.

One evening General Carr summoned me to his tent. He said he wanted to send some scouts with dispatches to Fort Supply, to be forwarded from there to General Sheridan. He ordered me to call the scouts together and to select the men who were to go.

I asked if I were to go, but he replied that he could not spare me. The distance to Camp Supply was about two hundred miles. Because of the very cold weather it was sure to be a hard trip. None of the scouts were at all keen about undertaking it, but it was finally settled that "Wild Bill," "Little Geary," a half-breed, and three other scouts should carry the dispatches.

They took their departure the next day with orders to return as soon, as possible.

We scouted for several days along the Canadian River, finding no sign of Indians. The general then returned to camp, and soon our wagon-train returned with provisions from Fort Lyon. Our animals were in poor condition, so we remained in different camps along San Francisco Creek and on the North Fork of the Canadian till "Wild Bill" and his scouts returned from Fort Supply.

Among the scouts in Penrose's command were fifteen Mexicans. Among them and the Americans a bitter feud existed. When Carr united Penrose's command with his own, and I was made chief of scouts, this feud grew more intense than ever. The Mexicans often threatened to "clean us out," but they postponed the execution of the threat from time to time. At last, however, when we were all in the sutler's store, the long-expected fight took place, with the result that the Mexicans were severely beaten.

On hearing of the row, General Carr sent for "Wild Bill" and me. From various reports he had made up his mind that we were the instigators of the affair. After listening to what we had to say, however, he decided that the Mexicans were as much to blame as we were. It is possible that both "Wild Bill" and I had imbibed a few more drinks than we needed that evening.

General Carr said to me:

"Cody, there are plenty of antelopes in the country. You can do some hunting while we stay here." After that my time was spent in the chase, and I had fine success. I killed from twenty to twenty-five antelopes every day, and the camp was supplied with fresh meat.

When the horses and mules belonging to the outfit had been sufficiently recruited to travel, we returned to Fort Lyon, reaching there in March, 1869.

The command recruited and rested for thirty days before proceeding to the Department of the Platte, whither it had been ordered.

At my request, General Carr kindly granted me a month's leave of absence to visit my family in St. Louis. He instructed Captain Hays, our quartermaster, to let me ride my mule and horse to Sheridan, 140 miles distant. At Sheridan I was to take the train for St. Louis.

I was instructed to leave the animals in the quartermaster's corral at Fort Wallace until I should come back. Instead of doing this, I put them both in charge of my old friend Perry, the hotel-keeper at Sheridan.

After twenty days, pleasantly spent with my family at St.

Louis, I returned to Sheridan. There I learned that my horse and mule had been seized by the Government.

The quartermaster's agent at Sheridan had reported to General Bankhead, commanding at Fort Wallace, and to Captain Laufer, the quartermaster, that I had left the country and had sold the animals to Perry. Laufer took possession of the animals, and threatened to have Perry arrested for buying Government property. He refused to pay any attention to Perry's statement that I would return in a few days, and that the animals had merely been left in his care.

As soon as I found this out I proceeded to the office of the quartermaster's agent who had told this lie, and gave him the thrashing he richly deserved. When I had finished with him he hastened to the fort, reported what had happened, and returned with a guard to protect him.

Next morning, securing a horse from Perry, I rode to Fort Wallace and demanded my horse and mule from General Bankhead. I told him they were Quartermaster Hays's property and belonged to General Carr's command, and explained that I had obtained permission to ride them to Sheridan and return.

General Bankhead gruffly ordered me out of his office and off the reservation, declaring that if I didn't leave in a hurry he would have me removed by force.

I told him he might do this and be hanged, using, very possibly, a stronger expression. That night, while sleeping at the Perry House, I was awakened by a tap on my shoulder and was astonished to see the room filled with armed negro soldiers with their guns all pointed at me. The first word came from the sergeant.

"Now looka heah, Massa Bill; if you move we'll blow you off

de fahm, suah!" Just then Captain Ezekial entered, and ordered the soldiers to stand back.

"I'm sorry, Bill," he said, when I demanded to know what this meant. "But I've been ordered by General Bankhead to arrest you and bring you to Fort Wallace."

"All right," said I. "But you could have made the arrest without bringing the whole Thirty-eighth Infantry with you."

"I know that, Bill, but you've not been in a very good humor the last day or two, and we didn't know how you'd act."

I dressed hurriedly and accompanied the captain to Fort Wallace. When we reached there at two o'clock in the morning the captain said:

"Bill, I'm sorry, but my orders are to put you in the guardhouse."

I told him I did not blame him for carrying out orders, and was made a guardhouse prisoner for the first and only time in my life. The sergeant of the guard, who was an old friend from Captain Graham's company, refused to put me in a cell, kindly allowing me to sleep in his own bed, and in a few minutes I was sound asleep.

Captain Graham called to see me in the morning. He said it was a shame to lock me up, and promised to speak to the general about it. At guard-mount, when I was not summoned, I sent word to Captain Graham that I wanted to see General Bankhead. He sent back word that the general refused to have anything to do with me.

As it was impossible to send word to General Carr, I determined to send a dispatch direct to General Sheridan. I wrote out a long telegram, informing him of my difficulty. But when it was taken to the telegraph office for transmission the operator refused to send it at once. Instead he showed it to General Bankhead, who tore it up. When no reply came I went to the office, accompanied by a guard, and learned from the operator what he had done.

"See here, my young friend," said I, "this is a public telegraph line. I want my telegram sent, or there'll be trouble."

He knew very well it was his duty to send the dispatch. I rewrote it and gave it to him, with the money to pay for it. But before he made any effort to transmit it he called on General Bankhead and informed him of what I had said. Seeing that the dispatch would have to go through, the general sent for me.

"If I let you go, sir, will you leave the Post at once and not bother anyone at Sheridan?" he demanded.

"No, sir," I replied, "I'll do nothing of the kind. I'll remain in the guardhouse till I get an answer from General Sheridan."

"If I give you your horse and mule will you proceed at once to Fort Lyon?"

"No, sir; I have some bills to settle at Sheridan and some other business to transact."

"Well, sir, will you at least promise not to interfere any further with the quartermaster's agent at Sheridan?"

"I shall not trouble him any more, sir. I have had all I want from him."

General Bankhead thereupon sent for Captain Laufer and ordered him to turn the horse and mule over to me. In a few minutes I was on my way to Sheridan, and, having settled my business there, I proceeded to Fort Lyon, arriving there two days afterward. I related my adventures to General Carr, Major Brown, and the other officers, who were highly amused thereby. ❒

# Chapter–6.

When I returned to General Carr's command after my experience as a prisoner I was informed that the general had been waiting for me for two weeks.

"I'm glad you've come, Bill," said the general. "While we've been at this Post a number of valuable animals have been stolen, as well as many Government horses and mules. We think the thieves are still near the fort.

Fresh tracks have been found near Fort Lyon. Perhaps Bill Green, the scout who has been up there, can tell you something about them."

Sending for Green, I found that he had marked the place where he had lost the trail of the marauders.

Next morning, accompanied by Green, Jack Farley, and another scout, I set out after the horse-thieves.

While making a circuit about the tracks we had found leading away from the spot where Green discovered them, we found the trail of twelve animals— four mules and eight horses—in the edge of the sandhills.

From this point we had no trouble in trailing them down to the Arkansas River. This stream they had followed toward Denver, whither they were undoubtedly bound.

When we got within four miles of Denver we found that the thieves had passed four days before. I concluded that they had decided to dispose of the animals in Denver. I was aware that Saturday was the big auction day there, so we went to a hotel outside the town to await that day. I was too well known in the city to show myself there, for the thieves would have taken alarm had they learned of my presence.

Early Saturday morning we rode into the city and stabled our animals at the Elephant Corral. I secured a room in a hotel overlooking the corral, and took up a post of observation. I did not have to wait long.

A man, whom I recognized at once as Williams, one of our old packers, rode into the ring, mounted on Lieutenant Forbush's mule, and leading another Government mule. This mule had been recently branded, and over the "U.S." a plain "D B" had been stamped.

As the man's confederate did not appear I decided he was outside with the rest of the stolen animals.

When Mr. Forbush's mule was put up at auction I came down to the corral and walked through the crowd of bidders.

The packer saw me, and tried to get away, but I seized him firmly by the shoulder.

"I guess, my friend," said I, "that you'll have to go with me. Make any resistance and I'll shoot you on the spot!"

To the auctioneer and an inquisitive officer I showed my commission as a United States detective. With Farley and Green, who were close at hand, I took my prisoner three miles down the Platte. There we dismounted, and began preparations to hang our prisoner to a limb. We informed him that he could escape this fate only by telling us where his partner was hidden.

He at first denied having any partner, but when we gave him five minutes to live unless he told the truth, he said his pal was in an unoccupied house three miles farther down the river.

We took up our journey, and, coming in sight of the house, saw a number of animals grazing near it. As we rode to the door, another of our old packers, whom I recognized as Bill Bevins, stepped to the front door. I instantly covered him with my rifle and ordered him to throw up his hands before he could draw his revolver.

Looking through the house, we found saddles, pack-saddles, lariats, blankets, overcoats, and two Henry rifles. We returned with the whole outfit to Denver, where we lodged Williams and Bevins in jail. The next day we tied each man to a mule and started on the return journey.

At the hotel where we had stopped before making the arrests, we were joined by our man with the pack mule. That night we camped on Cherry Creek, seventeen miles from Denver.

It was April, and the weather was cold and stormy. We found a warm and cozy camping-place in the bend of the creek. We made our beds in a row— feet to the fire. The prisoners had thus far been docile and I did not think it necessary to hobble them. They slept inside, and it was arranged that some one was to be constantly on guard. About one o'clock in the morning it began snowing. Shortly before three, Jack Farley, who was on guard, and sitting at the foot of the bed with his back to the prisoners, was kicked into the fire by Williams. The next instant Bevins, who had got hold of his shoes, sprang up, jumped over the fire, and started away on the run.

As soon as I was enough awake to comprehend what was going on I sent a shot after him. Williams attempted to follow Bevins, but as he did so I knocked him down with the butt of my revolver. Farley had by this time got out of the fire. Green had started after Bevins, firing at him as he ran, but the thief made his escape into the brush.

In his flight, unfortunately for him, he dropped one of his shoes.

Leaving Williams in charge of Farley and "Long Doc," the man with the pack mule, Green and I struck out for Bevins. We heard him breaking through the brush, but, knowing it would be useless to try to follow him on foot, we went back and saddled two of the fastest horses. At daylight we struck out on his trail, which was plainly visible in the snow.

Though he had an hour and a half's start his track lay through a country covered with prickly pear. We knew that with a bare foot he could make little progress. We could see, however by the long jumps he was taking, that he was making excellent time. Soon the trail became spotted with blood, where the thorns of the prickly pear had pierced his shoeless foot.

After a run of twelve miles we saw Bevins crossing a ridge two miles ahead. We reached the ridge just as he was descending the divide toward the South Platte, which at this point was very deep and swift.

If he got across the stream he stood a good chance of escape. We pushed our horses as fast as possible, and when we got within range I told him to halt or I would shoot. He knew I was a good shot, and coolly sat down to wait for us.

"Bevins, you gave us a good chase," I said, as we rode up.

"Yes," he returned calmly, "and if I'd had fifteen minutes' more start and got across the Platte you'd never have caught me."

Bevins's flight was the most remarkable feat of its kind I have ever heard of. A man who could run barefooted in the snow through a prickly-pear patch was surely a "tough one." When I looked at the man's bleeding foot I really felt sorry for him. He asked me for my knife, and when I gave it to him he dug the thorns out of his foot with its sharp point. I consider him the gamest man I ever met.

I could not suffer a man with such a foot to walk, so I dismounted, and he rode my horse back to camp, while Green and I rode the other horse by turns. We kept a close watch on our prisoner. We had had plenty of proof that he needed it. His injured foot must have pained him fearfully, but never a word of complaint escaped him.

After breakfasting we resumed our journey. We had no further trouble till we reached the Arkansas River, where we found a vacant cabin and took possession of it for the night.

There was no fear that Bevins would try to escape. His foot was swollen to a great size, and was useless. Believing that Williams could not get away from the cabin, we unbound him.

The cabin was comfortably warmed and well-lighted by the fire. We left "Long Doc" on guard and went to sleep.

At one o'clock Williams asked "Doc" to allow him to step to the door for a minute. "Doc" had his revolver in hand, and did not think it necessary to waken us. He granted the request. With "Doc," revolver in hand, watching him, Williams walked to the outer edge of the floor. Suddenly he made a spring to the right and was out of sight in the black darkness before his guard could even raise his revolver.

"Doc" leaped after him, firing just as he rounded the corner of the cabin. The report brought us all to our feet. I at once covered Bevins with my revolver, but, seeing that he could barely stir, I lowered it.

Then in came "Doc," swearing a blue streak and announcing

that Williams had escaped. Nothing was left us but to gather our horses close to the cabin and stand guard the rest of the night to prevent the possibility of our late prisoner sneaking in and getting away with one of them. This was the last I ever saw or heard of Williams, but we got back to Fort Lyon with Bevins.

Though we had lost one of our prisoners, General Carr complimented us on the success of our trip. The next day we took Bevins to Bogg's Ranch, on Picket Wire Creek, where he was to await trial. But he never was tried. He made his escape, as I had expected he would do.

In 1872 I heard that he was at his old tricks on Laramie Plains. A little later he sent word to me that if he ever met me he would kill me on sight. Shortly thereafter he was arrested and convicted for robbery, but made his escape from Laramie City prison. Later he organized a desperate gang of outlaws which infested the country north of the Union Pacific. When, the stage began running between Cheyenne and Deadwood, these outlaws robbed coaches and passengers, often making big hauls of plunder. Finally most of the gang were caught, tried, and convicted, and sent to the penitentiary for a number of years. Bevins was among the number.

Soon after my return to Fort Lyon, the Fifth Cavalry was ordered to the Department of the Platte. While we were at Fort Wallace, getting supplies en route I passed the quarters of General Bankhead, who had ordered my arrest on the occasion of my last visit to that Post. The general sent out for me, and as I entered his office he extended his hand.

"I hope you have no hard feelings for me, Cody," he said. "I have just had a talk with General Carr and Quartermaster Hays. If you had told me you had permission to ride that horse and mule, there would have been no trouble."

"That's all right, General," I said. "I don't believe your quartermaster's agent will ever circulate any more false stories about me."

"No," said the general; "he hasn't recovered yet from the beating you gave him."

When the command reached the north fork of the Beaver, I rode down the valley toward the stream, and discovered a large fresh Indian trail. I found tracks scattered all over the valley and on both sides of the creek, as if a large village had recently passed that way. I estimated there could not be less than four hundred lodges, or between twenty-five hundred and three thousand warriors, women, and children in the band.

When I reported my discovery to General Carr, he halted his regiment, and, after consulting a few minutes, ordered me to select a ravine, or as low ground as possible, so that the troops might be kept out of sight of the Indians until we could strike the creek.

We went into camp on the Beaver. The general ordered Lieutenant Ward to take twelve men and myself and follow up the trail for several miles. Our orders were to find out how fast the Indians were traveling. I soon made up my mind by the frequency of their camps that they were moving slowly, hunting as they journeyed.

After we had scouted about twelve miles, keeping our horses well concealed under the bank of the creek, Ward and I left our horses and crept to a high knoll where there was a good view for some distance down-stream. As we looked over the summit of the hill we saw a whole Indian village, not three miles away. Thousands of ponies were grazing on the prairie. To our left, on the opposite side of the creek, two or three parties of Indians were coming in, laden with buffalo meat.

"This is no place for us, Lieutenant," said I. "I think we have business at the camp which must be attended to as soon as possible."

"I agree with you," he returned. "The quicker we get there the better."

We came down the hill as fast as we could and joined our men. Lieutenant Ward hurriedly wrote a note and sent it to General Carr by a corporal. As the man started away on a gallop Ward said: "We will march, slowly back until we meet the troops. I think General Carr will soon be here."

A minute or two later we heard shots in the direction taken by our courier. Presently he came flying back around the bend of the creek, with three or four Indians in hot pursuit. The lieutenant, with his squad of soldiers, charged upon them. They turned and ran across the stream.

"This will not do," said Ward, when the last redskin had disappeared. "The whole village will know the soldiers are near by."

"Lieutenant," said I, "give me that note. I'll take it to the general."

He gladly handed me the dispatch. Spurring my horse, I dashed up the creek. Soon I observed another party of Indians returning to the village with meat. I did not wait for them to attack me, but sent a shot after them at long range.

In less than an hour I reached the camp and delivered the dispatch to General Carr. "Boots and Saddles" was sounded, and all the troops save two companies, which were left to guard the supply train, were soon galloping toward the Indian camp.

When we had ridden three miles we met Lieutenant Ward. He had run into a party of Indian hunters. One of their number had been killed in the encounter, and one of Ward's horses had been wounded.

At the end of five miles we came in sight of hundreds of Indians, advancing up the creek to meet us.

They formed a complete line on our front. General Carr, who wanted to strike their village, ordered the troops to charge, break through the line, and keep straight on.

No doubt this movement would have been successfully executed had it not been for the daredevil, rattle-brained Lieutenant Schinosky, commanding Company B. Misunderstanding the orders, he charged on the Indians on the left, while the rest of the command swept through the line. The main body was keeping straight on toward the village when it was discovered that Schinosky and his company were surrounded by five hundred Indians.

To save the company, General Carr was forced to order a halt and hurry back to the rescue. During the short fight Schinosky had several men and a number of horses killed.

Valuable time had been consumed by the rescue. Night was coming on. The Indians were fighting desperately to keep us from reaching their village, whose population, having been informed by courier of what was going on, was packing up and getting away.

During the afternoon we had all we could do to hold our own with the mounted warriors. They stayed stubbornly in our front, contesting every inch of ground.

The wagon-train, which had been ordered to come up, had not arrived. Fearful that it had been surrounded, General Carr ordered the command to return and look for it. We found it at nine o'clock that night, and went into camp.

Next morning, when we moved down the creek, not an Indian was to be seen. Village and all, they had disappeared. Two miles down the stream we came to a spot where the village had been located. Here we found many articles which had been left in the hurry of flight. These we gathered up and burned.

The trail, which we followed as rapidly as possible, led northeast toward the Republican River. On reaching that stream a halt was ordered. Next morning at daylight we again pulled out. We gained rapidly on the Indians, and could occasionally see them from a distance.

About eleven o 'clock that morning, while Major Babcock was ahead with his company, and as we were crossing a deep ravine, we were surprised by perhaps three hundred warriors. They at once began a lively fire. Our men galloped out of the ravine to the rough prairie and returned it. We soon succeeded in driving the enemy before us. At one time we were so close upon them that they threw away most of their lodges and camp equipment, and left their played-out horses behind them. For miles we could see Indian furniture strewn in all directions.

Soon they scattered into small bodies, dividing the trail. At night our horses began to give out, and a halt was called. A company was detailed to collect all the loose Indian ponies, and to burn the abandoned camp equipment.

We were now nearly out of rations. I was sent for supplies to the nearest supply point, old Fort Kearney, sixty miles distant.

Shortly after this the command reached Fort McPherson, which for some time thereafter continued to be the headquarters of the Fifth Cavalry. We remained there for ten days, fitting out for a new expedition. We were reënforced by three companies of the celebrated Pawnee Indian Scouts, commanded by Major Frank North. At General Carr's recommendation I was now made chief of scouts in the Department of the Platte, with better pay. I had not sought this position.

I became a firm friend of Major North and his officers from the start. The scouts had made a good reputation for themselves. They had performed brave and valuable services in fighting against the Sioux, whose bitter enemies they were. During our stay at Fort McPherson I made the acquaintance of Lieutenant George P. Belden, known as "The White Chief." His life has been written by Colonel Brisbin, of the army. Belden was a dashing rider and an excellent shot. An hour after our introduction he challenged me to a rifle match, which was at once arranged.

We were to shoot ten shots each at two hundred yards for fifty dollars a side. Belden was to use a Henry rifle. I was to shoot my old "Lucretia." This match I won. Belden at once proposed another, a hundred-yard match, as I was shooting over his distance. This he won. We were now even, and we stopped right there.

While we were at Fort McPherson, General Augur and Brevet-Brigadier- General Thomas Duncan, colonel of the Fifth Cavalry, paid us a visit for the purpose of reviewing our command. The men turned out in fine style, and showed themselves to be well-drilled soldiers. Next the Pawnee scouts were reviewed. It was amusing to see them in their full uniform. They had been supplied with the regular cavalry uniform, but on this occasion some of them had heavy overcoats, others large black hats with all the brass accoutrements attached; some were minus trousers and wore only breech-clouts. Some had regulation pantaloons, but only shirts. Part of them had cut the breech of their pantaloons away, leaving only the leggings. Still others had big brass spurs, but wore no boots nor moccasins.

But they understood the drill remarkably well for Indians. The commands were given them by Major North, who spoke their tongue as readily as any full-blooded Pawnee. They were well mounted, and felt proud of the fact that they were regular United States soldiers. That evening after the drill many ladies attended the dance of the Indians. Of all savages I have ever seen, the Pawnees are the most accomplished dancers.

Our command set out on the trail the next day. Shortly afterward, when we were encamped on the Republican River near the mouth of the Beaver, we heard the yells of Indians, followed by shots, in the vicinity of our mule herd, which had been driven down to water.

Presently one of the herders, with an arrow still quivering in his flesh, came dashing into the camp.

My horse was close at hand. Mounting him bareback, I galloped after the mule herd, which had been stampeded. I supposed that I would be the first man on the scene. But I found I was mistaken. The Pawnee scouts, unlike regular soldiers, had not waited for the formality of orders from their officers. Jumping their ponies bareback and putting ropes in the animals' mouths, they had hurried to the place from which the shots came and got there before I did.

The marauders proved to be a party of fifty or more Sioux, who had endeavored to stampede our animals. They were painfully surprised to find their inveterate enemies, the Pawnees, coming toward them at full gallop. They had no idea the Pawnees were with the command. They knew that it would take regular soldiers a few minutes to turn out, and fancied they would have plenty of time to stampede the herd and get away.

In a running fight of fifteen or twenty miles several of the Sioux were killed. I was mounted on an excellent horse Colonel Royal had selected for me. For the first mile or two I was in advance of the Pawnees. Soon a Pawnee shot past me. I could not help admiring the horse he was riding. I determined that if possible that horse should be mine. He was a big buckskin, or yellow horse. I took a careful look at him, so as to recognize him when we got back to camp.

After the chase was over I rode over to Major North and asked him about the animal. I was told that he was one of the favorite steeds of the command.

"What chance is there to trade for him?" I asked.

"It is a Government horse," replied the Major. "The Indian who rides him is very much attached to him."

I told Major North I had fallen in love with the horse, and asked if he had any objections to my trying to secure him. He replied that he had not. A few days later, after making the Indian several presents, I persuaded him to trade horses with me. In this way I became possessed of the buckskin, although he still remained Government property. I named him Buckskin Joe, and he proved to be a second Brigham.

I rode him during the summers of '69, '70, '71, and '72. He was the horse ridden by the Grand Duke Alexis on his buffalo hunt. In the winter of '72, after I had left Fort McPherson, Buckskin Joe was condemned and sold at public sale to Dave Perry at North Platte. In 1877 he presented him to me. He remained on my ranch on the Dismal River for many years, stone blind, until he died.

At the end of twenty days, after a few unimportant running fights, we found ourselves back to the Republican River.

Hitherto the Pawnee scouts had not taken much interest in me. But while at the camp I gained their respect and admiration by showing them how to kill buffaloes. Though they were excellent buffalo killers, for Indians, I had never seen them kill more than four or five animals in one run. A number of them would surround a herd and dash in on it, each one killing from one to four buffaloes. I had gone out in company with Major North, and watched them make a "surround." Twenty Pawnees, circling a herd, killed thirty-two buffaloes.

As they were cutting up the animals, another herd appeared. The Pawnees were getting ready to surround it, when I asked Major North to keep them back to let me show them what I could do. He did as I requested. I knew Buckskin Joe was a good buffalo horse, and, feeling confident that I would astonish the Indians, I galloped in among the herd. I did astonish them. In less than a half-mile run I dropped thirty-six, killing a buffalo at nearly every shot. The dead animals were strung out over the prairie less than fifty feet apart. This manner of killing greatly pleased the Indians. They called me "Big Chief," and thereafter I had a high place in their esteem.

We soon left the camp and took a westward course up the Republican River. Major North, with two companies of his Pawnees, and Colonel Royal, with two or three companies of cavalry, made a scout north of the river.

After making camp on the Blacktail Deer Fork we observed a band of Indians coming over the prairie at full gallop, singing and yelling and waving their lances and long poles. We first supposed them to be the hostile Sioux, and for a few moments all was excitement. But the Pawnees, to our surprise, made no effort to go out to attack them. Presently they began singing themselves. Major North walked over to General Carr and said:

"General, those are our men. They had had a fight. That is the way they act when they come back from battle with captured scalps."

The Pawnees came into camp on the run. We soon learned that they had run across a party of Sioux who were following a big Indian trail. The Sioux had evidently been in a fight. Two or three had been wounded, and were being carried by the others. The Pawnees "jumped" them, and killed three or four of their number.

Next morning our command came up to the Indian trail where the Sioux had been found. We followed it for several days. From the number of campfires we passed we could see that we were gaining on the Sioux.

Wherever they had camped we found the print of a woman's shoe. This made us all the more eager to overtake them, for it was plain that they had a white woman as their captive.

All the best horses were selected by the general, and orders were given for a forced march. The wagon-train was to follow as rapidly as possible, while the command pushed on ahead.

I was ordered to pick out five or six of the best Pawnees and proceed in advance of the command, keeping ten or twelve miles ahead, so that when the Indians were overtaken we could learn the location of their camp, and give the troops the required information in time to plan an effective attack.

When we were ten miles in advance of the regiment we began to move cautiously. We looked carefully over the summits of the hills before exposing ourselves to observation from the front. At last we made out the village, encamped in the sandhills south of the South Platte River at Summit Springs.

Here I left the Pawnees to watch, while I rode back to the command and informed General Carr that the Indians were in sight.

The men were immediately ordered to tighten their saddles and otherwise to prepare for action. I changed my horse for old Buckskin Joe. He had been led for me up to this time, and was comparatively fresh. Acting on my suggestion, General Carr made a circuit to the north. I knew that if the Indians had scouts out they would naturally watch in the direction whence they had come. When we had passed the camp, and were between it and the river, we turned and started back.

By this maneuver we avoided detection by the Sioux scouts. The general kept the command wholly out of sight until within a mile of the village. Then the advance guard was halted till all the soldiers caught up. Orders were issued that at the sound of the charge the whole command was to rush into the village.

As we halted on the summit of the hill overlooking the still unsuspecting Sioux, General Carr called to his bugler:

"Sound the charge!"

The bugler, in his excitement, forgot the notes of the call. Again the general ordered "Sound the charge!" and again the musician was unable to obey the command.

Quartermaster Hays, who had obtained permission to join the command, comprehended the plight of the bugler. Rushing up to him, he seized the bugle, and sounded the call himself, in clear, distinct tones. As the troops rushed forward he threw the bugle away, and, drawing his pistol, was among the first to enter the village. The Indians had just driven up their horses and were preparing to move camp when they saw the soldiers.

Many of them jumped on their ponies, and, leaving everything behind them, advanced to meet the attack. On second thought, however, they decided it would be useless to resist. Those who were mounted rode away, while those on foot fled for the neighboring hills. We charged through their village, shooting right and left at everything we saw. Pawnees, officers, and regular soldiers were all mixed together, while the Sioux went flying away in every direction.

The general had instructed the soldiers to keep a sharp lookout for white women when they entered the village. Two were soon found. One of them was wounded, and the other had just been killed. Both were Swedes, and the survivor could not speak English.

A Swedish soldier was soon found to act as interpreter. The woman's name was Weichel. She said that as soon as the Indians saw the troops coming, a squaw, the wife of Tall Bull, had killed Mrs. Alerdice, her companion in captivity, with a hatchet. The infuriated squaw had attacked Mrs. Weichel, wounding her. The purpose of the squaw was apparently to prevent both women from telling the soldiers how cruelly they had been treated.

The attack lasted but a little while. The Indians were driven several miles away. The soldiers gathered in the herd of Indian horses, which was running wild over the prairie, and drove the animals back into camp. After a survey of our work we found we had killed about one hundred and forty Indians and captured one hundred and twenty squaws and papooses, two hundred lodges, and eight hundred horses and mules.

General Carr ordered that all the tepees, lodges, buffalo robes, camp equipage, and provisions, including a large quantity of buffalo meat, should be gathered and burned. Mrs. Alerdice, the murdered Swedish captive, was buried. Captain Kane read the burial service, as we had no chaplain with us. While this was going on, the Sioux warriors recovered from their panic and came back to give us battle. All around the attack a fight began. I was on the skirmish line, and noticed an Indian who was riding a large bay horse, and giving orders to his men in his own language.

I could understand part of what he said. He was telling them that they had lost everything and were ruined, and was entreating them to follow him until they died. The horse this chief was riding was extremely fleet. I determined to capture him if possible, but I was afraid to fire at the rider lest I kill the horse.

Often the Indian, as he rode around the skirmish line, passed the head of a ravine. It occurred to me that if I dismounted and crept up the ravine, I could, as he passed, easily drop him from the saddle with no fear of hitting the horse. Accordingly I crept into the ravine and secreted myself there to wait till Mr. Chief came riding by.

When he was not more than thirty yards away I fired. The next instant he tumbled from the saddle, and the horse kept on his way without a rider. Instead of running back to the Indians, he galloped toward the soldiers, by one of whom he was caught.

Lieutenant Mason, who had been very conspicuous in the fight and had killed two or three Indians himself, came galloping up the ravine, and, jumping from his horse, secured the elaborate war-bonnet from the head of the dead chief, together with all his other accoutrements.

We both rejoined the soldiers. I started in search of the horse, and found him in the possession of Sergeant McGrath, who had captured him. McGrath knew that I had been trying to get the horse, and he had seen me kill its rider. He handed the animal over to me at once. I little thought at the time that I had captured the fastest running horse west of the Missouri River, but this later proved to be the fact.

Late that evening our wagon-train arrived. Mrs. Weichel, the wounded woman, had been carefully attended by the surgeons, and we placed her in the ambulance. Gathering up the prisoners, squaws, and papooses, we set out for the South Platte River, eight miles distant, where we went into camp.

Next morning, by order of General Carr, all the money

found in the village was turned over to the adjutant. Above two thousand dollars was collected, and the entire amount was given to Mrs. Weichel.

The command now proceeded to Fort Sedgwick, from which point the particulars of our fight, which took place Sunday, July 11, 1869, was telegraphed to all parts of the country.

During our two weeks' stay at this Post, General Augur, of the Department of the Platte, made us a visit, and complimented the command highly on the gallant service it had performed. Tall Bull and his Indians had long been a terror to the border settlements. For their crushing defeat, and the killing of the chief, General Carr and the command were complimented in General Orders.

Mrs. Weichel was cared for in the Post hospital. After her recovery she married the hospital steward. Her former husband had been killed by the Indians. Our prisoners were sent to the Whetstone Agency, on the Missouri, where Spotted Tail and the friendly Sioux were then living. The captured horses and mules were distributed among the officers and soldiers.

Among the animals which I thus obtained were my Tall Bull horse and a pony which I called Powder Face. This animal figured afterward in the stories of "Ned Buntline," and became famous.

One day, while we were waiting at Fort McPherson, General Carr received a telegram announcing that the Indians had made a dash on the Union Pacific, killing several section men and running off stock of O'Fallen's Station. An expedition was going out of Fort McPherson to catch and punish the redskins if possible.

I was ordered by General Carr to accompany this expedition. That night I proceeded by rail to Fort McPherson Station, and from there rode horseback to the fort. Two companies, under command of Major Brown, had been ordered out. Next morning, as we were about to start, Major Brown said to me:

"By the way, Cody, we're going to have a character with us on this scout. It's old 'Ned Buntline,' the novelist."

At the same time I saw a stoutly built man near by who wore a blue military coat. On his breast were pinned perhaps twenty badges of secret societies and gold medals. He limped a little as he approached me, and I concluded that this must be the novelist.

"He has a good mark to shoot at on his left breast," I said to Brown, "but he looks like a soldier." I was introduced to him by his real name, which was Colonel E.Z.C. Judson.

"I was to deliver a temperance lecture tonight," said my new acquaintance, "but no lecture for me when there is a prospect of a fight. The major has offered me a horse, but I don't know how I shall stand the ride."

I assured him that he would soon feel at home in the saddle, and we set out. The command headed for the North Platte, which had been swollen by mountain rains. In crossing we had to swim our horses. Buntline was the first man across.

We reached O'Fallen's Station at eleven o'clock. In a short time I succeeded in finding an Indian trail. The party of Indians, which had come up from the south, seemed to be a small one. We followed the track of the Indians, to the North Platte, but they had a start of two days. Major Brown soon abandoned the pursuit, and returned to Fort Sedgwick. During this short scout, Buntline had plied me with questions. He was anxious to go out on the next scout with me.

By this time I had learned that my horse, Tall Bull, was a remarkably fast runner. Therefore, when Lieutenant Mason, who owned a racer, challenged me to a race, I immediately accepted. We were to run our horses a single dash of a half mile for five hundred dollars a side.

Several of the officers, as well as Rube Wood, the post-trader, offered to make side bets with me. I took them up until I had my last cent on Tall Bull.

I saw from the start that it would be easy to beat the lieutenant's horse, and kept Tall Bull in check, so that no one might know how fast he really was. I won easily, and pocketed a snug sum. Everybody was now talking horse race. Major Brown said that if Tall Bull could beat the Pawnees' fast horse, I could break his whole command.

The next day all the troops were paid off, including the Pawnees. For two or three days our Indian allies did nothing but run horses, as all the lately captured animals had to be tested to determine which was the swiftest.

Finally the Pawnees offered to run their favorite against Tall Bull. They raised three hundred dollars to bet on their horse, and I covered the money. In addition I took numerous side bets. The race was a single dash of a mile. Tall Bull won without any trouble, and I was ahead on this race about seven hundred dollars.

I also got up a race for my pony, Powder Face, against a fast pony belonging to Major Lute North, of the Pawnee Scouts. I selected a small boy living at the Post for a jockey, Major North rode his own pony. The Pawnees, as usual, wanted to bet on their pony, but as I had not yet ascertained the running qualities of Powder Face I did not care to risk much on him. Had I known him as well as I did afterward I would have backed him with every cent I had. He proved to be one of the swiftest ponies I ever saw, and had evidently been kept as a racer.

The dash between the ponies was to be four hundred yards. When I led Powder Face over the course he seemed to understand what he was there for. North was on his pony; my boy was up. I had all I could do to hold the fiery little fellow back. He was so lively on his feet that I feared his young rider might not be able to stick on his back.

At last the order to start was given by the judges. I brought Powder Face up to the score, and the word "Go!" was given. So swiftly did he jump away that he left his rider sitting on the ground. Nevertheless he went through and won the race without a rider. It was an easy victory, and after that I could get no more races.

General Carr having obtained a leave of absence, Colonel Royal was given command of an expedition that was ordered to go out after the Indians. In a few days we set out for the Republican, where, we had learned, there were plenty of Indians.

At Frenchman's Fork we discovered a village, but did not surprise it, for the Indians had seen us approaching and were in retreat as we reached their camping-place.

We chased them down-stream and through the sandhills, but they made better time than we did, and the pursuit was abandoned.

While we were in the sandhills, scouting the Niobrara country, the Pawnee Indians brought into camp some very large bones, one of which the surgeon of the expedition pronounced to be the thigh bone of a human being. The Indians said the bones were those of a race of people who long ago had lived in that country. They said these people were three times the size of a man of the present day, that they were so swift and strong that they could run by the side of a buffalo, and, taking the animal in one arm, could tear off a leg and eat it as they ran.

These giants, said the Indians, denied the existence of a Great Spirit. When they heard the thunder or saw the lightning, they laughed and declared that they were greater than either. This so displeased the Great Spirit that he caused a deluge. The water rose higher and higher till it drove these proud giants from the low grounds to the hills and thence to the mountains. At last even the mountaintops were submerged and the mammoth men were drowned.

After the flood subsided, the Great Spirit came to the conclusion that he had made men too large and powerful. He therefore corrected his mistake by creating a race of the size and strength of the men of the present day. This is the reason, the Indians told us, that the man of modern times is small and not like the giants of old. The story has been handed down among the Pawnees for generations, but what is its origin no man can say.

❐

# Chapter–7.

One morning, in the spring of 1870, a band of horse-stealing Indians raided four ranches near the mouth of Fremont Creek, on the North Platte. After scooping up horses from these ranches they proceeded to the Fort McPherson herd, which was grazing above the Post, and took about forty Government animals. Among these was my favorite little pony, Powder Face.

When the alarm was given, "Boots and Saddles" was sounded. I always kept one of my best horses by me, and was ready for any surprise. The horse that I saddled that day was Buckskin Joe.

As I galloped for the herd, I saw the Indians kill two of the herders. Then, circling all the horses toward the west, they disappeared over a range of hills. I hurried back to the camp and told the general that I knew where to pick up the trail. Company I, commanded by a little red-headed chap— Lieutenant Earl D. Thomas—was the first to report, mounted, at the adjutant's office. Thomas had but lately graduated from West Point.

His sole instructions were: "Follow Cody and be off quick." As he rode away General Emory called after him: "I will support you with more troops as fast as they are saddled."

The lieutenant followed me on the run to the spot where I saw the Indians disappear. Though the redskins had an hour and a half start on us, we followed them, on a gallop, till we could see that they had begun to drive their horses in a circle, and then in one direction after another, making the trail uncertain. It was getting dark, but I succeeded in keeping on some of the tracks.

All that night the Indians endeavored, by scattering their horses, to throw us off the trail. At three o'clock in the morning I made up my mind that they were traveling for the headwaters of Medicine Creek, and headed straight in that direction.

We found that they had reached the creek, but remained there only long enough to water their horses. Then they struck off to the southwest. I informed Lieutenant Thomas that the next water was at the Springs at the head of Red Willow Creek, thirty-five miles away. The Indians, I said, would stop there.

Thomas's men had not had time to bring so much as their coats with them. At the alarm they grabbed their sidearms and carbines and ammunition belts, and leaped into their saddles. None of us had had anything to eat since dinner the day before. In the whole outfit there was not a canteen in which to carry water.

I notified Thomas that he must decide whether the troop was to undergo the terrible hardship of riding a whole day without food or water, on the chance of overtaking the Indians and getting their rations and supplies away from them. He replied that the only instructions he had received from General Emory were to follow me. I said that if it were left to me, I would follow the Indians.

"You have heard Cody," said Thomas to his men. "Now, I would like to hear what you men think about it."

Through their first sergeant they said they had followed Cody on many a long trail, and were willing to follow him to the end of this one. So the order to mount was given, and the trail was taken up. Several times that day we found the Indians had resorted to their old tactics of going in different directions. They split the herd of horses in bunches, and scattered them. It was very hard to trail them at good speed.

Forty hours without food, and twelve hours without water, we halted for a council when darkness set in.

I told Thomas that when we got within three miles of the Springs the men could rest their horses and get a little sleep, while I pushed on ahead to look for the Indians. This was done. When we reached the spot I had designated the saddles were removed, so that the horses could graze and roll. I rode on ahead.

As I had suspected I should, I found the Indians encamped at the Springs with the stock grazing around them. As quickly as possible I got back to the command with my news. The horses were quietly saddled and we proceeded, seldom speaking or making any noise.

As we rode along I gave the lieutenant and first sergeant the description of the camp and suggested that it could be best approached just at daylight. We had but forty-one men. Ten of these, I said, should be detailed to take charge of the herd, while the lieutenant and I charged the camp.

The Indians were encamped on a little knoll, around which was miry ground, making a cavalry charge difficult. The Indians numbered as many as we did. The safest plan was to dismount some of the men, leaving others to hold the horses, and proceed to the attack on foot. The rest of the men were to remain with their horses, and get through, the marshy ground mounted, if they could.

A halt was called, and this was explained to the men. It didn't take them long to understand. We approached very cautiously till we got within a quarter of a mile of the Indians. Then the charge was sounded. We did not find the land as miry as we had supposed. Dashing in among the Indians, we completely surprised them. Most of them grabbed the guns, with which they always slept, and fled to the marsh below the camp. Others ran for their horses. It was fortunate that we had dismounted ten men. These were able to follow the Indians who had escaped to marsh.

When we made the charge my chief thought was to keep a lookout for my pony, Powder Pace. Soon I saw an Indian, mounted on him, making his escape. I rushed through the camp, shooting to the left and right, but keeping a beeline after Powder Face and his rider. Soon another Indian who was afoot leaped up behind Powder Face's rider. I knew that the little animal was very swift for a short distance, but that he would be badly handicapped by the weight of two men.

I realized that my old Buckskin Joe was tired but his staying qualities were such that I was sure he would overtake Powder Face, carrying double weight.

Though I was not a hundred yards behind the object of my pursuit when the second Indian mounted I was afraid to shoot. It was not yet quite daylight. I feared to fire lest I hit my beloved pony. For two miles I followed through the sandhills before I dared to use my rifle.

The Indian riding at the rear had a revolver with which he kept banging away, but I paid little attention to him. I knew a man shooting behind with a pistol was likely to hit nothing but air. At last I took a steady aim while old Joe was running smoothly. The bullet not only hit the rear man, but passed through him and killed the man in front.

They both fell. I took another shot to make sure they were not playing 'possum. As they fell, Powder Face stopped and looked around, to learn what it was all about. I called to him, and he came up to me.

Both Indians were wearing beautiful war-bonnets, of which I took possession, as well as of their fancy trappings. Then, taking Powder Face by the rope, I led him back to the Springs to see how the lieutenant had made out.

The herd of horses was held and surrounded by a few soldiers. The rest were still popping at the Indians. But most of the redskins were either hidden among the marshes, or had got clear away to the surrounding hills.

I found the lieutenant, and told him I thought we had accomplished all that was possible. The orderly sounded the recall. I have never seen a muddier set of boys than those who came out of the marsh and began rummaging around the Indian camp. We soon discovered two or three hundred pounds of dried meat—buffalo, deer, and antelope, also a little coffee and sugar and an old kettle and tin cups which the Indians had used.

All the men by this time had all the water they wanted. Each was chewing a piece of dried meat. Pickets were posted to prevent a surprise. Soon coffee was ready. In a short time everybody was filled up, and I told Thomas we had better be getting out of there.

Many of the men began saddling the stolen horses, so as to rest their own. The lieutenant was eager to remain and rest until the reënforcements that General Emory had promised should arrive.

"Your orders were to follow me, weren't they?" I asked. "Yes."

"Well, then, keep on following me, and you'll soon see the reason for getting out of here."

"All right," he agreed. "I've heard the general say that in a tight place your directions should always be followed."

With most of the men driving the captured horses we started for Fort McPherson. I didn't take the trail that we had followed in. I knew of a shorter route, and besides, I didn't want to meet the support that was coming. I knew the officer in command, and was sure that if he came up he would take all the glory of the capture away from Lieutenant Thomas.

Naturally I wanted all the credit for Thomas and myself as we were entitled to.

The soldiers that had been sent out after us found and destroyed the village, but we did not meet them. They discovered seven or eight dead Indians, and there were a few more down in the marsh which they overlooked. The major in command sent out scouts to find our trail. Texas Jack, who was on this duty, returned and reported that he had found it, and that we were going back to the fort by another route.

The major said: "That's another of those tricks of Cody's. He will guide Thomas back and he will get all the glory before I can overtake him."

We rode into Fort McPherson about six o'clock that evening. I told Thomas to make his report immediately, which he did. General Emory complimented him highly, and Thomas generously said that all he did was to obey orders and follow Cody. A report was made to General Sheridan, and the next day that officer wired Thomas his congratulations.

The next day the command that was sent out after us returned to the fort. The major was hotter than a wounded coyote. He told the general that it was all my fault, and that he did not propose to be treated in any such manner by any scout, even if it were General Sheridan's pet, Buffalo Bill. He was told by the general that the less he said about the matter the better it would be for him. This was Lieutenant Thomas's first raid, and he was highly elated with its success. He hoped he would be mentioned for it in Special Orders, and sure enough, when the Special Orders came along both he and myself, together with the little command, received complimentary mention. This Thomas richly deserved, for he was a brave, energetic, and dashing officer. I gave him the two war-bonnets I had taken from the Indians I shot from the back of Powder Face, asking that he present them to the daughters of General Augur, who were then visiting the Post.

Shortly after our return another expedition was organized, with the Republican River country as its destination. It was commanded by General Duncan, a blusterer, but a jolly old fellow. The officers who knew him well said we would have a fine time, as he was very fond of hunting. He was a good fighter. It was rumored that an Indian's bullet could never hurt him. A cannon-ball, according to report, had hit him in the head without injuring him at all, while another cannon-ball, glancing off his skull, had instantly killed one of the toughest mules in the army!

The Pawnee scouts, who had been mustered out of service during the winter of 1869 and '70, were reorganized to accompany this expedition. I was glad of this. I had become very much attached to Major North, one of the officers, and to many of the Indians. Beside myself the only white scout we had in the Post at this time was John Y. Nelson, whose Indian name was Cha-Sha-Cha-Opeyse, or Red-Willow-Fill-the-Pipe. The man was a character. He had a squaw wife and a half-breed family. He was a good fellow, but had few equals and no superiors as a liar.

With the regimental band playing "The Girl I Left Behind Me" we started out from the Post. A short march brought us to the head of Fox Creek, where we camped. Next morning General Duncan sent me word that I was to bring my rifle and shoot at a mark with him. I did not feel like shooting at anything except myself, for the night before I had been interviewing the sutler's store, in company with Major Brown. When I looked for my gun, I found that I had left it behind me. I got cold consolation from Major Brown when I informed him of my loss. Then I told him that the general had sent for me to shoot a match with him, and that if the old man discovered my predicament there would be trouble.

"Well, Cody," said the major, "the best thing you can do is to make some excuse, and then go and borrow a gun from one of the men. Tell the general you loaned your rifle to someone for a hunt. While you are gone I will send back to the Post for it."

I got a gun from John Nelson, and marched to the general's headquarters, where I shot the match. It resulted in his favor.

General Duncan, who had never before commanded the Pawnee Scouts, confused them by posting the guards in a manner that was new to them. Furthermore, he insisted that the guards should call the hours through the night: "Nine o'clock and all is well," etc., giving the numbers of their posts. Few of the scouts understood English. They were greatly troubled.

Major North explained to them that when the man on the post nearest them called the hour, they must repeat the call as closely as they could. It was highly amusing to hear them do this. They would try to remember what the man on the next post had said. For example, when a white soldier called out "Post Number One, Half-past Nine and all is well!" the Indians would cry out "Poss Number half-pass five cents go to h—l I don't care." So ridiculous were their efforts to repeat the calls, that the general finally gave it up and countermanded the order.

One day, after an uneventful march, Major North and I went out on Prairie Dog Creek in advance of the command to kill some buffaloes. Night was approaching, and we looked about for a suitable camping-place for the soldiers. Major North dismounted and was resting, while I rode down to the creek to see if there was plenty of grass in the vicinity.

I found an excellent camping spot, and told North I would ride over the hill a little way, so that the advance guard might see me. This I did, and when the advance guard came in sight I dismounted and lay down upon the grass to rest.

Suddenly I heard three or four shots. In a moment Major North came dashing toward me, pursued by eight or ten Indians. I at once sprang to the saddle and sent several shots toward the Indians, fifty or more of whom were now in sight. Then, we turned our horses and ran.

The bullets sang after us. My whip was shot from my hand, and the daylight was let through the crown of my hat. We were in close quarters, when Lieutenant Valknar, with several men, came galloping to our relief. The Indians, discovering them, whirled and fled.

As soon as Major North sighted his Pawnees he began riding in a circle, which was the signal to them that there were hostile Indians in front. In an instant they broke ranks pell-mell, with the major at their head, and went after the flying warriors.

The second day that we had been following the Indians we came upon an old squaw who had been left on the prairie to die. Her people had built for her a little shade or lodge, and had given her some provisions—enough to last her trip to the Happy Hunting-Grounds. This is often done by the Indians when an enemy is in pursuit and one of their number becomes too feeble to keep pace with the flight.

Our scout, John Nelson, recognized the squaw as a relative

of his Indian wife. From her we learned that the redskins we were pursuing were known as the Pawnee Killer band. They had lately killed Buck's surveying party, consisting of eight or nine men. This massacre had occurred a few days before on Beaver Creek. We had found a number of surveying instruments in the abandoned camp, and knew therefore that the Indians had had a fight with white men. After driving the Indians across the Platte we returned to Fort McPherson, bringing with us the old squaw, who was sent to the Spotted Tail Agency.

During my absence my wife had given birth to a son. Though he was several weeks old when I returned no name had been given him. I called him Elmo Judson, in honor of Colonel Judson, whose pen name was "Ned Buntline." But the officers insisted upon calling him Kit Carson Cody and it was finally settled that this should be his name.

Shortly after my return I received orders instructing me to accompany Professor Marsh on a fossil-hunting expedition into the rough lands of the Big Horn Basin. The party was to consist of a number of scientists besides Professor Marsh, together with twenty-five students from Yale, which institution was sending out the expedition.

I was to get together thirty-five saddle-horses for the party. The quartermaster arranged for the transportation, pack mules, etc. But General Sheridan, under whose direction the scientists were proceeding, always believed in my ability to select good horses from a quartermaster's herd.

In a few days Professor Marsh and his companions arrived. The Pawnee Scouts, then in camp, had a year before unearthed some immense fossil bones, so it was decided that Major North, with a few of these scouts, should also accompany the expedition. Professor Marsh had heard of this discovery, and was eager to find some of the same kind of fossils.

Professor Marsh believed that the Basin would be among the last of the Western lands to be settled. The mountain wall which surrounded it would turn aside pioneers going to Montana or northern Oregon. These would head to the east of Big Horn Mountains, while those bound for Utah, Idaho, and California would go to the south side of the Wind River Mountains. He was confident, however, that some day the Basin would be settled and developed, and that in its fertile valleys would be found the most prosperous people in the world. It was there that my interest in the great possibilities of the West was aroused.

I never forgot what I heard around the campfire. In 1894 the Carey Irrigation Act was passed by Congress. A million acres of land was given to each of the arid States. I was the first man to receive a concession of two hundred thousand acres from the Wyoming State Land Board.

I could not get away to the Basin till late in the autumn of 1894, so I formed a partnership with George T. Beck, who proceeded to Wyoming, where he was found by Professor Elwood Mead, then in the service of the State.

There a site was located and the line of an irrigation canal was surveyed.

A town was laid out along the canal, and my friends insisted upon naming it Cody. At this time there was no railroad in the Big Horn Basin; but shortly afterward the Burlington sent a spur out from its main line, with Cody as its terminus. In 1896 I went out on a scout to locate the route of a wagon road from Cody into the Yellowstone Park. This was during Mr. McKinley's first administration.

I went to Washington, saw the President, and explained to him the possibilities of a road of eighty miles, the only one entering the National Park from the East. It would be, I told him, the most wonderful scenic road in the West. Mr. Roosevelt ordered the building of this road, which has now become the favorite automobile route into the Park. Today the Big Horn Basin is one of the richest of American oil lands, and the Pennsylvania of the West for coal production. Every one of the prophecies that Professor Marsh made to us around that campfire has come true.

In December, 1870, I was sent as a witness to Fort D.A. Russell, near the city of Cheyenne, where a court-martial was to be held. Before leaving home my wife had given me a list of articles she needed for the furnishing of our house. These I promised to purchase in Cheyennc.

On arriving at Fort Russell I found many officers, also witnesses at the court-martial, and put in most of my time with them. A postponement of a week gave us an opportunity to "do" Cheyenne. That town furnished abundant opportunities for entertainment, as there was every kind of game in operation, from roulette to horse-racing. I sent for my horse, Tall Bull, and a big race was arranged between him and a Cheyenne favorite called Green's Colt. But before Tall Bull could arrive the court-martial was over and the race was off. I sold the animal to Lieutenant Mason. I met many old friends in Cheyenne, among them R.S. Van Tassell, Tim Dier, Major Talbot, Luke Morrin, Posey Wilson, and many others. They constituted a pretty wild bunch, and kept me so busy that I had no time to think about Mrs. Cody's furniture.

On my return, when she asked us for it, I told her I couldn't bring it with me on the train, and that moreover there were no stores in Cheyenne where I could get furniture that would be good enough for her, so I had sent to Dewey & Stone at Omaha for what she needed.

I lost no time in getting over to the club, where I wrote to

Dewey & Stone for all the articles my wife required. In a week the furniture arrived at Fort McPherson station. I got a couple of six-mule teams and went after it quick. When it arrived at the house and was unpacked Mrs. Cody was greatly delighted.

About this time General Emory was very much annoyed by petty offenses in the vicinity of the Post by civilians over whom he had no jurisdiction. There was no justice of the peace near the Post, and he wanted some kind of an officer with authority to attend to these troublesome persons. One day he told me that I would make an excellent justice.

"You compliment me too highly, General," I replied. "I don't know any more about law than a Government mule knows about bookkeeping." "That doesn't make any difference," he said. "I know you will make a good squire. You accompany Mr. Woodin and Mr. Snell to North Platte in my private ambulance. They will go on your bond, and you will be appointed a justice of the peace."

A number of officers from the Post went to North Platte for this occasion. After I was duly sworn in, there was a celebration. I arrived home at three o'clock in the morning, Mrs. Cody still being in ignorance of my newly acquired honor. I was awakened by hearing her arguing with a man at the door who was asking for the squire. She was assuring him that no squire was on the premises.

"Doesn't Buffalo Bill live here?" asked the man.

"Yes," admitted Mrs. Cody, "but what has that got to do with it?"

By this time I had dressed, and I went to the door. I informed my wife, to her amazement, that I was really a squire, and turned to the visitor to learn his business.

He was a poor man, he said, on his way to Colorado. The

night before a large bunch of horses was being driven past his camp, and one of his two animals was driven off with the herd. Mounting the other, he followed and demanded the horse, but the boss of the herd refused to give it up. He wanted a writ of replevin.

I asked Mrs. Cody if she could write a writ of replevin and she said she had never heard of such a thing. I hadn't either.

I asked the man in, and Mrs. Cody got breakfast for us. He refused the drink I set out for him. I felt that I needed a good deal of bracing in this writ of replevin business, so I drank his as well as mine.

Then I buckled on my revolver, took down my old Lucretia rifle, and, patting her gently, said: "You will have to be constable for me today."

To my wife and children, who were anxiously watching these proceedings, I said:

"Don't be alarmed. I am a judge now, and I am going into action. Come on, my friend," I said to the stranger, "get on your horse."

"Why," he protested, "you have no papers to serve on the man, and you have no constable."

"Don't worry," I said. "I'll soon show you that I am the whole court."

I mounted Joe, and we galloped along about ten miles when we overtook the herd of horses. I found the boss, riding a big gray horse ahead of the herd. I ordered him to round up the herd.

"By what authority!" he demanded. "Are you a constable?"

I said I was not only a constable, but the whole court, and one of his men at the same time whispered to him: "Be careful, that is Buffalo Bill!" At this time, as well as for years past, I had been chief United States detective for the army as well as scout and guide. I felt that with the offices of justice and constable added to these titles I had all the power necessary to take one horse.

The herd boss evidently thought so, too. After asking if my name were Cody, and being told that it was, he said:

"Well, there is no need of having a fuss over one horse."

"No," said I, "a horse doesn't mean much to you, but it amounts to a good deal to this poor immigrant."

"Well," said the herd boss, "how do you propose to settle it?"

"I am going to take you and your whole outfit to Fort McPherson. There I am going to try you and give you the limit—six months and a five-hundred- dollar fine."

"I can't afford to go back to the Fort," he pleaded, "let's settle it right here. What will you take to call it off?"

"One hundred and fifty dollars," I said, "and quick!"

Reaching down into his pocket, he pulled out a wallet filled with bills and counted out a hundred and fifty dollars. By this time the man who had lost the horse had caught his animal in the herd. He was standing, holding it, near by.

"Partner," I said to him, "take your horse and go back home."

"Now, boss," I said to the other man, "let me give you a little advice. Be careful when a stranger gets into your herd and the owner overtakes you and demands it. You may run into more trouble than I have given you, for you ought to know by this time that horse-stealing is a hanging offense."

He said: "I didn't care a blank about your being justice of the peace and constable combined, but when I found out you were Buffalo Bill it was time to lay down my hand."

"All right, old fellow," I said, "good-by."

As he rode off he called: "It was worth a hundred and fifty dollars just to get a good look at you," and the other men agreed.

By the time I got back to the fort, guard-mount was over, and a number of officers were in the club. When they learned how I had disposed of my first case, they told the general, who was very much pleased.

"I want it noised about among the outside civilians how you handle your court," he said. The story soon became known all over the surrounding country. Even the ladies of the Post heard of it, and told my wife and sisters, to whom I had never mentioned it. They looked upon it as a great joke.

❒

# Chapter–8.

Early in the month of September, 1874, word was received at Fort McPherson that General Sheridan and a party of friends were coming to the Post to have a grand hunt in the vicinity. They further proposed to explore the country from Fort McPherson to Fort Hays in Kansas. They arrived in a special car at North Platte, eighteen miles distant, on the morning of September 22.

In the party besides General Sheridan were James Gordon Bennett, of The New York Herald, Leonard Lawrence Jerome, Carroll Livingston, Major J.G. Heckscher, General Fitzhugh, General H.E. Davies, Captain M. Edward Rogers, Colonel J. Schuyler Crosby, Samuel Johnson, General Anson Stager, of the Western Union, Charles Wilson, editor of The Chicago Journal, Quartermaster-General Rucker, and Dr. Asch, of General Sheridan's staff.

They were met at the station by General Emory and Major Brown, with a cavalry company as escort and a sufficient number of vehicles to carry the distinguished visitors and their baggage.

At the Fort they found the garrison, under the command of General Carr, on parade awaiting their arrival.

A train of sixteen wagons was provided to carry the baggage supplies and forage for the hunting trip. Besides these there were three or four horse- ambulances in which the guns were carried, and in which members of the party might ride when they became weary of the saddle. I accompanied the expedition at the request of General Sheridan. He introduced me to everybody and gave me a good send-off. As it was a high-toned outfit I was to accompany, I determined to put on a little style myself. I dressed in a new suit of light buckskin, trimmed along the seams with fringe of the same material. I put on a crimson shirt, elaborately decorated on the bosom, and selected a big sombrero for my head. Then, mounting a showy horse which was a gallant stepper, I rode down to the fort, rifle in hand.

The expedition was soon under way. First in line rode General Sheridan, followed by his guests; then the orderlies. Then came the ambulances, in one of which were carried five greyhounds, brought along to course antelopes and rabbits.

With the ambulance marched a pair of Indian ponies belonging to Lieutenant Hayes, captured during an Indian fight. These were harnessed to a light wagon, which General Sheridan occasionally used. These little animals, thirteen hands high, showed more vigor and endurance than any we brought with us.

During our first night in camp the members of the party asked me hundreds of questions about buffaloes and buffalo hunting. The entire evening was spent in talk about buffaloes, together with stories of the Plains, the chase, and the war, which was then fresh in the minds of all of us. We closed the evening by christening the camp, Camp Brown, in honor of the gallant officer who was in command of the escort.

We breakfasted at four the next morning and at six we were in the saddle. Everyone was eager to see the buffaloes which I had promised would be met with during the day. After a march of five miles the advance guard which I commanded sighted six of these animals grazing about two miles away.

Acting upon my suggestion, Lawrence Jerome, Livingston, Heckscher, Fitzhugh, Rogers, and Crosby, with myself as guide, rode through a convenient cañon to a point beyond the herd, and to windward of them; the rest of the party made a detour of nearly five miles, keeping behind the crest of a hill.

We charged down on the buffaloes at full gallop, and just then the other party emerged from their concealment and witnessed the exciting chase.

The buffaloes started away in a line, single file; Fitzhugh, after a lively gallop, led us all. Soon he came alongside the rear buffalo, at which he fired. The animal faltered, and with another shot Fitzhugh brought him to the ground. Crosby dashed past and leveled another of the herd, while Livingston dropped a third. Those who were not directly engaged in the hunt now came up and congratulated the buffalo killers. Fitzhugh was hailed as the winner of the Buffalo Cup. There was general sympathy for Heckscher, whose horse had fallen and rolled over him, thus putting him out of the race.

The hunt being over, the column moved forward through a prairie-dog town, several miles in extent. Thesc animals are found throughout the Plains, living together in a sort of society. Their numberless burrows in their towns join each other and the greatest care is necessary in riding among them, since the ground is so undermined as easily to give way under the weight of a horse.

Around the entrance to each burrow earth is piled to the height of at least a foot. On these little elevations the prairie-dogs sit on their haunches, chattering to each other and observing whatever passes on the Plains.

They will permit a person to approach very closely, but when they have viewed him they dive into their holes with wonderful celerity. They are difficult to kill. If hit they usually succeed in getting underground before they can be recovered.

Rattlesnakes and little owls are found in great numbers in the prairie-dog towns, living in the same burrows. We killed and cooked a few of the prairie- dogs, and found them very palatable.

A short distance beyond the prairie-dog town we found a settlement of five white men. They Proved to be the two Clifford brothers, Arthur Ruff, Dick Seymour, and John Nelson. To the last I have already referred. Each of these men had a squaw for a wife and numerous half-breed children. They lived in tents of buffalo skins. They owned a herd of horses and a few cattle, and had cultivated a small piece of land. Their principal occupation was hunting, and they had numbers of buffalo hides, which they had tanned in the Indian fashion.

Upon reaching Pleasant Valley on Medicine Creek the party divided into two detachments, one hunting along the bank of the creek for elk and deer, the other remaining with the main body of the escort.

The elk hunters met with no success whatever, but the others found plenty of buffaloes and nearly everybody killed one before the day was done.

Lawrence Jerome made an excellent shot. He was riding in an ambulance, and killed a buffalo that attempted to cross the line of march. Upon crossing the Republican River on the morning of the twenty-sixth we came upon an immense number of buffaloes scattered over the country in every direction. All had an opportunity to hunt. The wagons and troops moved slowly along toward the next camp while the hunters rode off in twos and threes. Each hunter was rewarded with abundant success.

Lawrence Jerome met with the only mishap. He was riding

Buckskin Joe, which I had lent him, and, dismounting to get a steady shot, thoughtlessly let go of the bridle.

The horse decided to do a little hunting on his own account. When last seen that day he was ahead of the buffaloes, and gaining, while his late rider was left to his own reflections. Three days later Joe, saddled and bridled, turned up at Fort McPherson.

We pitched our camp for the night in a charming spot on the bank of Beaver Creek. The game was so abundant that we remained there the next day. This stopping-place was called Camp Cody, in honor of the reader's humble servant. The next day was spent in hunting jack-rabbits, coyotes, elk, antelope, and wild turkeys.

That we had a splendid dinner may be seen from the following

BILL OF FARE

Soup

Buffalo Tail

Fish

Broiled Cisco; Fried Dace

Entrées

Salmi of Prairie Dog; Stewed Rabbit; Filet of Buffalo aux Champignons

Vegetables

Sweet Potatoes, Mashed Potatoes, Green Peas

Dessert

Tapioca Pudding

Wines

Champagne Frappé, Champagne au Naturel, Claret, Whisky, Brandy, Ale Coffee

I considered this a fairly good meal for a hunting party. Everybody did justice to it.

The excursionists reached Fort Hays on the morning of October second. There we pitched our tents for the last time. That same afternoon General Sheridan and his guests took the train for the East. They expressed themselves as highly pleased with the hunt, as well as with the way they had been guided and escorted.

General Davies afterward wrote the story of this hunt in a volume of sixty- eight pages, called "Ten Days on the Plains." In this chapter I have taken the liberty of condensing frequently from this volume, and in some cases have used the general's exact language. I ought to insert several lines of quotations marks, to be pretty generally distributed through the foregoing account.

After the departure of General Sheridan's party we returned to Fort McPherson, and found General Carr about to start on a twenty days' scout. His object was more to take some friends on a hunt than to look for Indians. His guests were a couple of Englishmen and Mr. McCarthy of New York, the latter a relative of General Emory. The command consisted of three companies of the Fifth Cavalry, one company of Pawnee Scouts, and twenty-five wagons. Of course I was called to accompany the expedition.

One day, after we had been out for some little time, I arranged with Major North to play a joke on Mr. McCarthy. I took him out on a hunt about eight miles from the camp, informing Major North about what time we should reach there. He had agreed that he would appear in the vicinity with his Indians, who were to throw their blankets around them and come dashing down upon us, firing and whooping in the true Indian style.

This program was faithfully carried out. I had been talking about Indians to McCarthy, and he had become considerably excited, when just as we turned a bend in the creek we saw a band of them not half a mile away. They instantly started after us on the gallop, yelling and shooting.

"McCarthy," said I, "shall we run or fight?"

He did not wait to reply. Wheeling his horse, he started at full speed down the creek. He lost his gun and dropped his hat, but never once did he look back to see if he were pursued. I tried to stop him by shouting that the Indians were Pawnees and our friends. He did not hear me, but kept straight on, never stopping his horse till he reached the camp.

I knew he would tell General Carr that the Indians had jumped him, and that the general would at once start out with troops. So as soon as the Pawnees rode up, I told them to remain there while I rode after my friend.

When I had reached camp, he had given the alarm, and the general had ordered out two companies of cavalry to go in pursuit of the Indians.

I told the general the Indians were only Pawnees, and that a joke had been put up on McCarthy. I neglected to tell him who had put up the joke. He was fond of a joke himself, and did not get very angry. I had picked up McCarthy's hat, which I returned to him. It was some time before it was discovered who was at the bottom of the affair.

It was while I was stationed at Fort McPherson, where Brevet-Major-General W.H. Emory was in command, that I acted as guide for Lord Flynn, an English nobleman who had come over for a hunt on the Plains. I had been recommended to him by General Sheridan.

Flynn had served in India with the British army. He was a fine sportsman and a splendid shot, and secured many heads and skins while he was with me.

Money meant little to him. He insisted on paying all the bills, spending his money lavishly on both officers and men when he was at the Post.

Once, when we ran out of liquid refreshments while on the hunt, we rode thirty miles to a saloon, only to find it closed. Lord Flynn inquired the price of the place, found it to be $500 and bought it. When we left, after having had all we needed to drink, he gave it—house, bar, stock, and all—to George Dillard, who had come along with the party as a sort of official bartender.

Sir George Watts-Garland also made a hunt with us. He was an excellent hunter and a thorough gentleman, but he lacked the personality that made Lord Flynn one of the most popular visitors who ever came to the Post.

Early in January, 1872, General Forsythe and Dr. Asch, of General Sheridan's staff, came to Fort McPherson to make preparations for a grand buffalo hunt to be conducted for the Grand Duke Alexis. General Sheridan was desirous of giving the Russian nobleman the hunt of his life. He wanted everything ready when the Grand Duke arrived, so that he need lose no time at the Post.

By way of giving their distinguished guest a real taste of the Plains, the two officers asked me to visit the camp of the Sioux chief, Spotted Tail, and ask him to bring a hundred of his warriors to the spot on Red Willow Creek, which, at my suggestion, had been selected as the Grand Duke's camp.

Spotted Tail had permission from the Government to hunt buffalo, a privilege that could not be granted to Indians indiscriminately, as it involved the right to carry and use firearms. You couldn't always be sure just what kind of game an Indian might select when you gave him a rifle. It might be buffalo, or it might be a white man. But Spotted Tail was safe and sane.

Hence the trust that was reposed in him.

Forsythe and Asch, after accompanying me to the site I had found for the camp, returned to the Post, while I set out to confer with Mr. Spotted Tail. The weather was very cold, and the journey was by no means a delightful one. I was obliged to camp out with only my saddle-blankets to protect me from the weather, and only my vigilance to protect me from the Indians.

Spotted Tail himself was friendly, but some of his young men were decidedly hostile. My activities as a scout had made me many enemies among the Sioux, and it is not their nature easily to forget old grudges.

At the close of the first day I made camp on a tributary of Frenchman's Fork, and built a little fire. The night was bitter cold, and I was so busy keeping warm that I got very little sleep. The next afternoon I began to notice fresh horse tracks and the carcasses of recently killed buffaloes. I knew that I was nearing an Indian camp. It was not policy to ride boldly in among the Indians, as some of them might be inclined to shoot me first and discover later that I was a friend of Spotted Tail. So I hid my horse in a low ravine and crawled up a hill, from whose summit I obtained a good view of the country.

When night fell, I rode into camp unobserved. As I entered the camp I wrapped my blanket, Indian fashion, about my head, so that the redskins would not at once recognize me as a white man. Then I hunted about till I found Spotted Tail's lodge. The old chief was stretched lazily out on a pile of robes as I looked in. He knew who I was and invited me to enter.

In the lodge I found Todd Randall, an old white frontiersman, who was Spotted Tail's friend and agent, and who had lived a great many years with the Indians. Randall, who spoke the Sioux jargon perfectly, did the interpreting, and through him I readily communicated to the chief the object of my visit.

I said that the warriors and chiefs would greatly please General Sheridan if they would meet him in about ten sleeps at the old Government crossing at the Red Willow. I said that a great chief from far across the water was coming to visit them, and that he was especially anxious to meet the greatest of the Indian chiefs.

Spotted Tail replied that he would be very glad to go. He added that on the morrow he would call his men together and select from them those who were to accompany him. He told me I had acted very wisely in coming first to him, as it was known to him that some of his young men did not like me, and he knew that they had hasty tempers. He expressed himself as pleased that they had not met me outside the village, and I assured him that I was equally pleased that this was so.

The chief then called his squaw, who got me something to eat, and I passed the remainder of the night in his lodge. Having informed the old man that this was no ordinary occasion, and that he would be expected to do the job up right, I returned to the Post.

When the day set for the Grand Duke's arrival came there was a brave array at the station to meet him. Captain Hays and myself had five or six ambulances to carry his party, Captain Egan was on hand with a company of cavalry and twenty extra saddle-horses, and the whole population of the place was gathered to see the great man from Russia.

The train came in, and from it stepped General Sheridan. A fine figure of a man was towering above him. This was the visitor.

I was presented to the Grand Duke as Buffalo Bill, the man

who would have charge of the hunt. I immediately ordered up the saddle-horse I had selected for the nobleman, also a fine horse for General Sheridan. Both men decided to ride for a few miles before they took seats in the ambulances.

When the whole party was mounted they started south, Texas Jack acting as guide until such time as I could overtake them. The Grand Duke was very much interested in the whole proceeding, particularly in the Indians. It was noticed that he cast frequent and admiring glances at a handsome red- skinned maiden who accompanied old Spotted Tail's daughter. When we made camp my titled guest plied me with questions about buffaloes and how to kill them. He wanted to know whether a gun or a pistol was the proper weapon and whether I would be sure to supply him with a horse that was trained in buffalo hunting.

I told him that I would give him Buckskin Joe, the best buffalo horse in the country, and that all he would need to do would be to mount the animal and fire away every time he saw a buffalo.

At nine o'clock in the morning we were all galloping over the prairies in search of big game. I waited till everyone was ready, and then led the party over a little knoll that hid the herd from view. In a few minutes we were among the buffaloes.

Alexis first chose to use his pistol. He sent six shots in rapid succession after one bull, at a distance of only twenty feet, but he fired wildly, and did no damage whatever. I rode up to his side, and, his pistol having been emptied, gave him mine. He seized it and fired six more shots, but not a buffalo fell.

I saw that he was pretty sure to come home empty-handed if he continued this sort of pistol practice. So I gave him my old "Lucretia" and told him to urge his horse close to the buffaloes, and not to shoot till I gave him the word. At the same time I gave

Buckskin Joe a cut with my whip which sent him at a furious gallop to within ten feet of one of the biggest bulls in the herd.

"Now is your time," I shouted to Alexis. He fired, and down went the buffalo. Then, to my amazement, he dropped his gun, waved his hat in the air, and began talking to members of his suite in his native tongue, which I of course was totally unable to understand. Old Buckskin Joe was standing behind the horse that I was riding, apparently quite as much astonished as I was at this singular conduct of a man he had accepted in good faith as a buffalo hunter.

There was no more hunting for the Grand Duke just then. The pride of his achievement had paralyzed any further activity as a Nimrod in him. Presently General Sheridan came riding up, and the ambulances were gathered round. Soon corks were popping and champagne was flowing in honor of the Grand Duke Alexis and his first buffalo.

Many of the newspapers which printed accounts of the hunt said that I had shot the buffalo for the Grand Duke. Others asserted that I held the buffalo while the Grand Duke shot him. But the facts are just as I have related them.

It was evident to all of us that there could be little more sport for that day. At the request of General Sheridan I guided the Russians back to camp.

Several of the others in the party decided to indulge in a little hunt on their own account, and presently we saw them galloping madly over the prairie in all directions, with terrified buffaloes flying before them.

As we were crossing a stream on our way back to camp we ran into a small band that had been frightened by some of these hunters. They came sweeping across our path, not more than thirty feet away, and as they passed Alexis raised his pistol and fired generally into the herd. A buffalo cow fell.

It was either an extraordinary shot or a "scratch," probably the latter. The Duke was as much astonished as any of us at the result, but we gave him three rousing cheers, and when the ambulance came up we had a second round of champagne in honor of the prowess of our distinguished fellow hunter. I began to hope that he would keep right on killing buffaloes all the afternoon, for it was apparent that every time he dropped an animal a basket of champagne was to be opened. And in those days on the Plains champagne was not a drink that could be indulged in very often.

I took care of the hides and heads of the buffaloes the Grand Duke had shot, as he wanted them all preserved as souvenirs of his hunt, which he was now enjoying immensely. I also cut the choice meat from the cow that he had killed and brought it into camp. At supper he had the pleasure of dining on buffalo meat which he himself had provided.

Eight buffaloes were killed by Alexis during the three days we remained in camp. He spent most of his time in the saddle, and soon became really accomplished. After he had satisfied himself as to his own ability as a buffalo killer he expressed a desire to see how the Indians hunted them. He had never seen bows and arrows used in the pursuit of game. Spotted Tail, who had joined the hunt according to his promise, picked out some of his best hunters, and when Alexis joined them directed them to surround a herd.

They were armed with bows and arrows and lances.

I told the Grand Duke to follow one particularly skillful brave whose name was Two Lance, who had a reputation for being able to drive an arrow clear through the body of a bull. The Indian proved equal to his fame. He hauled alongside of an animal, and, bending his powerful bow, let fly an arrow, which passed directly through the bulky carcass of a galloping brute, who fell dead instantly. The arrow, at the Grand Duke's request, was given to him as a souvenir which he doubtless often exhibited as proof of his story when some of his European friends proved a little bit skeptical of his yarns of the Western Plains.

When the visitor had had enough of buffalo hunting, orders were given to return to the railroad. The conveyance provided for Alexis and General Sheridan was an old-fashioned Irish dogcart, drawn by four spirited cavalry horses. The driver was old Bill Reed, an overland-stage driver, and our wagon-master. The Grand Duke vastly admired the manner in which he handled the reins.

On the way over, General Sheridan told his guest that I too was a stage- driver, and Alexis expressed a desire to see me drive.

"Cody," called the general, "come back here and exchange places with Reed. The Grand Duke wants you to drive for a while."

In a few minutes I had the reins, and we were racing across the prairie. We jogged along steadily enough, despite a pretty rapid pace, and this did not suit General Sheridan at all.

"Shake 'em up a little, Bill," he told me as we were approaching Medicine Creek. "Show us some old-time stage-driving."

I gave the horses a sounding crack with the whip, and they jumped into their work with a real interest. The load was light and their pace increased with every second.

Soon they were fairly flying over the ground, and I had all I could do to maintain any control over them. At last we reached a steep hill, or divide, the further side of which sloped down to the creek. There was no brake on the wagon, and the four horses were not in the least inclined to hold back, appearing to be wholly unconcerned as to what might happen.

It was impossible to restrain them. My work was cut out for me in keeping them on the track. So I let them set their own pace down the hill. The wagon bounded and rebounded from the bumps in the road, and my two distinguished passengers had to keep very busy holding their seats.

However, when they saw that the horses were being kept in the road they assumed an appearance of enjoying themselves. I was unable to slacken the pace of the horses until they dashed into the camp where we were to obtain a relay. There I succeeded in checking them.

The Grand Duke and the general said they had got a lot of enjoyment out of the ride, but I noticed that thereafter they were perfectly willing to travel at an easier pace.

When we arrived at North Platte, the Grand Duke invited me into his car, and there, over a few bottles of champagne, we went over all the details of the hunt. He said the trip was one which he would never forget and professed himself as wholly unable to thank me for my part in it.

As I was leaving the car one of his suite approached me, and, extending a big roll of greenbacks, begged me to accept it as a slight token of the Grand Duke's appreciation of my services.

I told him I could take nothing for what I had done. He then handed me a small jewel box, which I slipped into my pocket without examining, and asked if I would not also accept the magnificent fur overcoat which Alexis had worn on the hunt.

I had frequently admired this coat, which was made of many fine Russian furs. I was glad to receive it as a remembrance from one of the most agreeable men I had ever guided on a hunting expedition.

After leaving us Alexis telegraphed to the most famous

of New York jewelers and had made for me a wonderful set of sleeve-links and a scarf- pin, studded with diamonds and rubies, each piece in the form of a buffalo head, as large as a silver half-dollar.

Reporters who accompanied the expedition telegraphed the story of this order to their New York newspapers. When later I arrived in New York, after this present had been given me, some of the papers said that Buffalo Bill had come to New York to buy a shirt on which to wear the jewelry given him by the Grand Duke Alexis.

Shortly after this, General Ord, who had accompanied the hunting party, rode over with me to Fort McPherson. On the way he asked me how I would like to have a commission in the regular army. General Sheridan, he said, had suggested that I ought to have a commission, and the matter could be arranged if I desired it.

I thanked the general, and asked him to thank General Sheridan. But though a commission was a tempting prize, I preferred to remain in the position I was holding. He said that if at any time I felt that I wanted a commission, I only needed to ask for it, and it would be given to me.

All I looked forward to was the life of the Plains. It was enough for me to be in the saddle, trusting each day to find some new adventure. Army life would mean a great deal of routine, and routine was something I could not endure.

So, giving up forever any hope of wearing an officer's shoulder-straps, I was about to turn back to the prairies to see what new opportunities for excitement offered, when a strange new call came to me.

General J.J. Reynolds, who had just arrived at Fort McPherson with the Third Cavalry, called me into the office one day and told me that he had a letter, railroad tickets, and five hundred dollars for me. Furthermore he informed me that a thirty days' leave of absence was awaiting me whenever I wanted to take it.

All this was the doing of the "Millionaires' Hunting Party," headed by James Gordon Bennett and the Jeromes, which I had guided the year before.

I was, in short, invited to visit my former charges in New York, and provided by them with money and mileage, and leisure for the trip.

❒

# Chapter–9.

Of course going to New York was a very serious business, and not to be undertaken lightly. The first thing I needed was clothes, and at my direction the Post tailor constructed what I thought was the handsomest suit in the world. Then I proceeded to buy a necktie, so that I could wear the present which had come in the little box from the Grand Duke—a handsome scarf-pin. The Grand Ducal overcoat and a new Stetson, added to the wardrobe I already possessed, completed my outfit. Almost everything I had was on my back, but just the same I borrowed a little trunk of my sister, so as to impress New York with the fact that I had as many clothes as any visitor from the West.

At the last minute I decided to take along my buckskin suit. Something told me that some of the people I had met in New York might want to know just how a scout looked in his business clothes. Mrs. Cody was much astonished because I did not ask for my brace of pistols, which had accompanied me everywhere I had gone up to that time.

She had great confidence in these weapons, which more than once had saved my life. She wanted to know what in the world I would do without them if I met any bad men in New York. I told her that I supposed there were policemen in New York whose business it was to take care of such people. Anyway, I was going to chance it.

On my arrival at Omaha I was met by a number of friends who had heard of my expected descent on New York. They drove me at once to the United States Court, where my old friend, Judge Dundee, was on the bench. The minute I entered the courtroom the judge rapped loudly with his gavel and said:

"This court is adjourned while Cody is in town." He joined the party, and we moved on to the Paxton Hotel, where a banquet was arranged in my honor.

I left for Chicago the next day. On arriving there, I was met at the depot by Colonel M.V. Sheridan, brother of General Philip Sheridan, my old friend and fellow townsman. "Mike" Sheridan, with his brother, the general, was living in a beautiful house on Michigan Avenue. There I met a number of the old officers with whom I had served on the Plains.

I was still wearing the wonderful overcoat that had been given me by the Grand Duke Alexis, and it was a source of continuous admiration among the officers, who pronounced it the most magnificent garment of its kind in America.

The splendor of the general's Michigan Avenue mansion was new to me; never before had I seen such vast rooms and such wonderful furnishings. It was necessary to show me how the gas was turned on and off, and how the water flowed in the bathroom. I moved around the place in a daze until "Mike," taking pity on me, escorted me to a barroom, where I was more at home. As we were partaking of a cocktail, a number of reporters from the Chicago papers came in. They had been told of my visit and plied me with questions. In the papers the next morning I found that I had had adventures that up to that time I had never heard of. The next evening I had my first adventure in high society, and it proved more terrifying to me than any Indian fight I had ever taken part in. Finding I had no proper raiment for a big ball, which was to be given in my honor, "Mike" Sheridan took me to the clothing department of Marshall Field's, where I was fitted with an evening suit.

The general's valet assisted me into these garments that evening. My long brown hair still flowed down over my shoulders and I was determined to go to the barber's and have it sheared before I made a public appearance, but General Sheridan would not hear of this. He insisted that I crown my long locks with a plug hat, but here I was adamant. I would go to the party in my Stetson or I would not go to the party at all.

The ball was held at the Riverside Hotel, which was then one of the fashionable hostelries of Chicago. When I was escorted in, I was told to give the colored boy my hat and coat—to this I violently objected. I prized the coat beyond all my earthly possessions and intended to take no chances with it. I was finally persuaded that the boy was a responsible employee of the hotel and reluctantly gave him the garment. Then I suffered myself to be led into the ballroom. Here I met a bevy of the most beautiful women I had ever seen. Fearing every minute that I would burst my new and tight evening clothes, I bowed to them all around—but very stiffly. To the general's request that I join in the next dance I entered a firm refusal. I knew no dances but square dances, so they got up an old-fashioned quadrille for me and I managed somehow to go through it. As soon as it was over, I hurriedly escorted my fair partner to her seat, then I quickly made my way to the barroom. The man behind the bar appreciated my plight. He stowed me away in a corner behind the icebox and in that corner I remained for the rest of the evening.

Several times the general and his friends came down to

"moisten up," and each time I heard them wondering aloud what had become of me. When the music stopped and the party broke up I emerged from my hiding-place. The next morning I reported to the general and explained to him that I was going back to the sagebrush. If New York were like Chicago, I wanted to be excused. But he insisted that I continue my trip.

At eleven o'clock the next morning he thrust me into a Pullman car, which was in charge of Mr. Angel, an official of the Pullman Car Company, and was taking a private party to the East.

Two of my millionaire hunting companions, J.B. Heckscher and Colonel Schuyler Crosby, met me at the station and drove me to the Union Club. That night I was told to put on my evening clothes and accompany them to a theater. Heckscher was very much disturbed when he saw the Chicago clawhammer that had been purchased for me.

"It will do for tonight," he said, "but tomorrow I'll send you to my tailor and have him make you some clothes fit for a gentleman to wear."

We saw Edwin Booth in a Shakespearean play. I was told that all my wealthy hunting friends would join me at breakfast the next morning. I was up at seven o'clock and waiting for them. The hours dragged slowly by and no guests arrived. I was nearly famished, but did not dare eat until the company should be assembled. About eleven o'clock, when I was practically starved, Mr. Heckscher turned up. I asked him what time they usually had breakfast in New York and he said about half-past twelve or any time therafter up to three.

At one, the gentlemen all made their appearance and were somewhat astonished at the amount of breakfast I stowed away, until they were told that I had been fasting since seven o'clock that morning.

During my visit to New York, I was taken by Mr. James Gordon Bennett to Niblo's Garden, where I saw "The Black Crook." We witnessed the performance from a private box and my breath was fairly taken away when the curtain went up on the fifth act. Needless to say, that was the first time I had ever witnessed a musical show and I thought it the most wonderful spectacle I had ever gazed upon.

The remainder of my visit in New York was spent in a series of dinners and theater parties. I was entertained in the house of each gentleman who had been with me on the hunt. I had the time of my life.

After I had had about all the high life I could stand for the time being I set out for Westchester, Pa., to find the only relative I knew in the East. My mother was born in Germantown. Her sister had married one Henry R. Guss, of Westchester.

I found on reaching Westchester that my relative was one of its most important citizens, having the Civil War title of general. I found his home with no trouble, and he was very delighted to see me. An old lady, who was a member of his household, he introduced to me as my grandmother. His first wife, my Aunt Eliza, was dead, and he had married a second time. He also introduced me to his son, Captain George Guss, who had been in the army with him during the Civil War.

It was not until we had talked of old family connections for an hour or more that they discovered that I was Buffalo Bill; then they simply flooded me with questions.

To make sure that I would return for a second visit, the young people of the family accompanied me back to New York. I was due for a dinner that evening, so I gave them a card to Mr. Palmer, of Niblo's Garden, and they all went to see "The Black Crook."

When I reached the club I was given a telegram from General Sheridan telling me to hasten to Chicago. He wanted me to hurry on to Fort McPherson and guide the Third Cavalry, under General Reynolds, on a military expedition. The Indians had been committing serious devastations and it was necessary to suppress them summarily. At the dinner, which was given by Mr. Bennett, I told my New York friends that I would have to leave for the West the next day. When the party broke up I went directly to the Albemarle Hotel and told my cousins that we would have to start early the next morning for Westchester. There I would remain twenty-four hours.

When we reached Westchester, my uncle informed me that they had arranged a fox hunt for the next morning, and that all the people in the town and vicinity would be present. They wanted to see a real scout and plainsman in the saddle.

Early next morning many ladies and gentlemen, splendidly mounted, appeared in front of my uncle's residence. At that time Westchester possessed the best pack of fox hounds in America. Captain Trainer, master of the hounds, provided me with a spirited horse which had on a little sheepskin saddle of a kind on which I had never ridden. I was familiar neither with the horse, the saddle, the hounds, nor fox-hunting, and was extremely nervous. I would have backed out if I could, but I couldn't, so I mounted the horse and we all started on the chase.

We galloped easily along for perhaps a mile and I was beginning to think fox- hunting a very tame sport indeed when suddenly the hounds started off on a trail, all barking at once. The master of the hounds and several of the other riders struck off across country on the trail, taking fences and stone walls at full gallop.

I noticed that my uncle and several elderly gentlemen stuck

to the road and kept at a more moderate gait. The eyes of the spectators were all on me. I don't know what they expected me to do, but at any rate they were disappointed. To their manifest disgust I stayed with the people on the road.

Shortly we came to a tavern and I went in and nerved myself with a stiff drink, also I had a bottle filled with liquid courage, which I took along with me. Just by way of making a second fiasco impossible I took three more drinks while I was in the bar, then I galloped away and soon overtook the hunters.

The first trail of the hounds had proved false. Two miles further on they struck a true trail and away they went at full cry. I had now got used to the saddle and the gait of my horse. I also had prepared myself in the tavern for any course of action that might offer.

The M.F.H. began taking stone walls and hedges and I took every one that he did. Across the country we went and nothing stopped or daunted me until the quarry was brought to earth. I was in at the death and was given the honor of keeping the brush.

At two o'clock that afternoon I took my departure for the West. Mr. Frank Thompson, of the Pennsylvania Railroad, who had ridden my famous buffalo horse, Buckskin Joe, on the great hunt, sent me to Chicago in his own private car.

At the station in Chicago I was met with orders from General Sheridan to continue straight ahead to Fort McPherson as quickly as possible. The expedition was waiting for me.

At Omaha a party of my friends took me off the train and entertained me until the departure of the next train. They had heard of my evening clothes and insisted on my arraying myself therein for their benefit. My trunk was taken to the Paxton Hotel and I put on the clawhammer and all that went with it. About fifty of my Omaha friends accompanied me to the train; in my silk hat and evening dress I was an imposing spectacle. But I expected to change into my Plains clothes as soon as I got into the car. However, these plans were sadly upset. Both my friends and I had forgotten my trunk, which in the hour of my greatest need was still reposing in a room in the Paxton Hotel, while in clothes fit only for a banquet I was speeding over the Plains to a possible Indian fight.

At Fort McPherson, my old friend, "Buffalo Chips," was waiting for me. He had been left behind by General Reynolds to tell me to overtake the command as soon as possible. He had brought out old Buckskin Joe for me to ride.

The expedition was already well on its way north into the Loup country and had camped at Pawnee Springs, about eight miles from McPherson Station, the night before.

Poor old Buffalo Chips almost fell dead when he saw how I was dressed. The hat especially filled him with amazement and rage, but there was nothing else to do. I had to go as I was or go not at all.

The champagne with which my Omaha friends had filled my stateroom I gave to the boys at the station. I did not have to urge them to accept it. They laughed a good deal at my stovepipe hat and evening dress, but because of the champagne they let me off without as much guying as I would otherwise have received.

Jumping on our horses, we struck out on the trail of the soldiers. It was about one o'clock when we overtook them. As we neared the rear guard, I pulled off my overcoat and strapped it behind my saddle. I also put my hair up under my stovepipe hat and galloped past the command, to all appearances fresh from a New York ballroom.

"Look at the dude! Look at the dude!" they shouted as I rode among them. Paying no attention to them, I galloped up and overtook General Reynolds. Saluting him, I said:

"General, I have come to report for duty."

"Who in thunder are you?" he demanded, looking at me without a sign of recognition in his eye.

"Why, general," I said, "I am to be your guide on this expedition." He looked at me a second time, and a grin spread over his face.

"Can it be possible that you are Cody?" he asked. I told him that I was Cody.

"Let down your hair," he commanded. I took off my hat, and my hair fell over my shoulders. A loud yell went up from both officers and enlisted men, as the word went up and down the line that the dude they had been bedeviling was none other than Buffalo Bill.

Texas Jack and the scouts who were ahead had heard the noise and came galloping back.

"Welcome back, old chief!" shouted Jack, and the scouts gathered around me, shaking my hand and congratulating me on my safe return from the dangers and the perils of the East.

The general asked me how far it was to the Loup Fork. I said it was about eight miles and offered to proceed there ahead of the command and select a good sheltered camp. This I did. The adjutant accompanying the detachment helped me and laid out the camping spot, and when the command pulled in they disposed themselves for the night in a beautiful grove of timber where there was plenty of firewood and good grass for the horses and mules. Soon the tents were up and big fires were crackling all around.

I accepted with thanks General Reynolds's invitation to mess with him on the trip. After dinner, before a big log fire, which was being built in front of the general's tent, the officers came up to meet me. Among those to whom I was introduced were Colonel Anthony Mills, Major Curtiss, Major Alexander Moore, Captain Jerry Russell, Lieutenant Charles Thompson, Quartermaster Lieutenant Johnson, Adjutant Captain Minehold, and Lieutenant Lawson. After this reception, I went down to visit the scouts in camp. There the boys dug me up all kinds of clothes, and clothes of the Western kind I very sadly needed.

White had brought along an old buckskin suit. When I had got this on and an old Stetson on my head, and had my favorite pair of guns strapped to me and my dear old "Lucretia Borgia" was within reach, I felt that Buffalo Bill was himself again.

The general informed me that evening that Indians had been reported on the Dismal River. At breakfast the next morning he said that a large war party had been committing devastations up and down the flat. His scouts had discovered their trail going north and had informed him that they would probably make camp on the Dismal. There they were sure to be joined by other Indians. He asked my opinion as to what had best be done.

I told him it was about twenty-five miles from the present tent to the Dismal River. I said I had better go on, taking White with me, and try to locate them.

"I've heard of this man White," said the general. "They tell me that he is your shadow and he follows you every place you go." I said that this was true and that I had all I could do to keep him from following me to New York. "It would break his heart," I said, "if I were to leave him behind now." I added that Texas Jack knew the country thoroughly and that he could guide the command to a point on the Dismal River where I could meet them that night. The general said:

"I have been fighting the Apaches in Arizona, but I find these Sioux are an entirely different crowd. I know little about them and I will follow your suggestions. You start now and I will have the command following you in an hour and a half."

I told White to get our horses at once and also to tell Texas Jack to report to me. When the latter reported I told him the general wanted him to guide the command to the course of the Dismal. When he got there, if he didn't hear from me in the meantime, he was to select a good camp.

White and I set out, riding carefully and looking for the trail. We had traveled about ten miles when I found it. The Indians were headed toward the Dismal. Presently another trail joined the first one, and then we had to begin extremely careful scouting.

I didn't follow the Indian trail, but bordered the left and struck the river about five miles above the Fork. There we turned down-stream. Soon on the opposite side we saw a party of Indians surrounding a herd of elk. I didn't approach them closely, neither did I follow down the stream any further. We kept parallel with the course of the river, and soon stopped at the foot of a high sandhill. From here I knew I could get a view of the whole country.

I told White to remain there until I came back, and, jumping off old Joe, I cautiously climbed the hill.

From behind a big soapweed—a plant sometimes called Spanish Dagger—I got a view of the Dismal River, for several miles. I immediately discovered smoke arising from a bunch of timber about three miles below me. Grazing around the timber were several hundred head of horses. Here I knew the Indian camp to be located.

I slipped down the hill, and, running to old Joe, mounted, telling White at the same time that I had located the camp. Then we began circling the sandhill until we got two or three miles away, keeping out of sight of the Indians all the time. When we felt we were safe we made a straight sweep to meet the command. I found the scouts first and told Texas Jack to hold up the soldiers, keeping them out of sight until he heard from me.

I went on until I met General Reynolds at the head of the column. He baited the troop on my approach; taking him to one side, I told him what I had discovered. He said:

"As you know the country and the location of the Indian camp, tell me how you would proceed."

I suggested that he leave one company as an escort for the wagon-train and let them follow slowly. I would leave one guide to show them the way. Then I would take the rest of the cavalry and push on as rapidly as possible to within a few miles of the camp. That done, I would divide the command, sending one portion across the river to the right, five miles below the Indians, and another one to bear left toward the village. Still another detachment was to be kept in readiness to move straight for the camp. This, however, was not to be done until the flanking column had time to get around and across the river.

It was then two o'clock. By four o'clock the flanking columns would be in their proper positions to move on and the charge could begin. I said I would go with the right-hand column and send Texas Jack with the left-hand column. I would leave White with the main detachment. I impressed on the general the necessity of keeping in the ravine of the sandhills so as to be out of sight of the Indians.

I said that, notwithstanding all the caution that we could take, we were likely to run into a party of hunters, who would immediately inform the camp of our presence. In case of discovery, I said, it would be necessary to make our charge at once.

General Reynolds called his officers together and gave them my suggestions as their instructions. In a very few minutes everything was moving. I accompanied Colonel Mills. His column had crossed the Dismal and was about two miles to the north of it when I saw a party of Indians chasing elk.

I knew that sooner or later—probably sooner—these Indians would see me. I told Colonel Mills he had better send the scout back to General Reynolds and make all haste to charge the village. We had no way of sending word to Major Curtiss, who led the other flanking column, and we had to trust to luck that he would hear the firing when it started.

Colonel Mills kept his troops on the lowest ground I could pick out, but we made our way steadily toward the village.

Inside of half an hour we heard firing up the river from where we were. Colonel Mills at once ordered his troops to charge. Luckily it collided with the Indians' herd of horses, which were surrounded, thus depriving most of the braves of their mounts.

Men were left to guard the animals, and, taking the rest of the company, we charged the village, reaching it a little after the arrival of General Reynolds. The attack was not as much a surprise as we had hoped for. Some of the Indian hunters had spied the soldiers and notified the camp, but General Reynolds, coming from the south, had driven all the Indians on foot and all the squaws and children toward the sandhills on the north. Mills came pretty near finding more Indians than he was looking for. Their force largely outnumbered ours when we collided, but Major Curtiss came charging down from the north just at this instant. His arrival was such a complete surprise that the Indians gave up and began waving the white flag. Then all firing ceased.

On rounding them up we found that we had captured about two hundred and fifty warriors, women, and children, most of whom were from the Spotted Tail Agency.

The general had the Indians instantly disarmed. Most of their tepees were up and they were ordered to go into them and remain there. We placed a sufficient guard around the whole camp so that none could escape. On the arrival of the wagon-train, for which a scout had been sent, the command went into camp.

Taking me aside, General Reynolds said:

"I want you to send one of your fastest men back to Fort McPherson. I am sending dispatches to General Ord, asking for instructions."

I selected White to make this trip, and he was ready for duty in five minutes.

We were then sixty-five miles from Fort McPherson Station. I told White that the matter was urgent and that he must get to that telegraph office as soon as possible. At ten o'clock the next morning he rode into our camp with a telegram to General Reynolds. The general was ordered to disarm all the Indians and send them under guard of a company of cavalry to the Spotted Tail Agency.

General Reynolds was very much delighted with the success of the expedition. On his arrival at the Fort he received congratulations from General Ord and from General Sheridan. General Sheridan asked in his telegram if Cody had gone along. The general wired back that Cody had gone along and also wrote a letter telling General Sheridan how he had reported in evening dress.

Of course the papers were soon full of this raid. Al Sorenson of the Omaha Bee, who had seen my evening clothes and silk hat in Omaha, wrote an extremely graphic story of my arrival on the Plains. I soon found that the officers and men in the Third Cavalry knew all about the incident.

During the spring of '72, the Indians were rather quiet. We did a little scouting, however, just to keep watch on them. One day, in the fall of that year, I returned from a scouting expedition, and as I passed the store there were a lot of men crowded in front of it. All of them saluted me with "How do you do, Honorable!" I rode straight to the general's private office. He also stood at attention and said:

"Good morning, Honorable."

"What does all this 'Honorable' mean, General?" I demanded. He said: "Of course, you have been off on a scout and you have not heard, but while you were gone you were nominated and elected to represent the twenty-sixth district of Nebraska in the Legislature." I said:

"That is highly complimentary, and I appreciate it, but I am no politician and I shall have to tender my resignation," and tender it I did.

My refusal to serve as a lawmaker was unqualified. I knew nothing about politics. I believe that I made a fairly good justice of the peace, but that was because of no familiarity with the written law. I merely applied the principles of fair-dealing to my cases and did as I would have been done by. The Golden Rule was the only statute I applied.

I inquired how to free myself formally from the new honors that had been thrust upon me, and soon another man was serving in my stead—and quite welcome he was to the pay and credit that might have been mine.

I returned back to the Plains for employment, but there was nothing to do. The Indians, for a wonder, were quiet. There was little stirring in the military posts. I could have continued to serve in one of them if I had chosen, and the way was still open to study for a commission as an officer. But army life without excitement was not interesting for me, and when Ned Buntline offered me a chance to come East and try my fortunes as an actor I accepted.

I accepted with misgivings, naturally. Hunting Indians across a stage differed from following them across the Plains. I knew the wild western Indian and his ways. I was totally unacquainted with the tame stage Indian, and the thought of a great gaping audience looking at me across the footlights made me shudder.

But when my old "pards," Wild Bill and Texas Jack, consented to try their luck with me in the new enterprise I felt better. Together we made the trip to New York, and played for a time in the hodgepodge drama written for us by Ned Buntline himself.

Before any of us would consent to be roped and tied by Thespis we insisted on a proviso that we be freed whenever duty called us to the Plains.

The first season was fairly prosperous, and so was the second. The third year I organized a "show" of my own, with real Indians in it—the first, I believe, who ever performed on a stage. I made money and began to get accustomed to the new life, but in 1876 the call for which I had been listening came.

The Sioux War was just breaking out. I closed the show earlier than usual and returned to the West. Colonel Mills had written me several times to say that General Crook wanted me to accompany his command. When I left Chicago I had expected to catch up with Crook at the Powder River, but I learned en route that my old command, the gallant Fifth Cavalry, was on its way from Arizona to join him, and that General Carr, my former commander, was at its head.

Carr wanted me as his guide and chief of scouts, and had written to army headquarters in Chicago to learn where I could be reached.

As soon as this news came to me I gave up the idea of overtaking Crook. I hastened to Cheyenne, where the Fifth Cavalry had already arrived, and was met at the depot there by Lieutenant Charles King, adjutant of the regiment, who had been sent by General Carr from Fort D.A. Russell. In later years, as General Charles King, this officer became a widely popular author, and wrote some of the best novels and stories of Indian life that I have ever read.

As I accompanied the lieutenant back to the fort, we passed soldiers who recognized me and shouted greetings. When we entered the Post a great shout of "Here's Buffalo Bill!" arose from the men on the parade ground. It was like old times, and I felt a thrill of happiness to be back among my friends, and bound for one of the regular old-time campaigns. The following morning the command pulled out for Fort Laramie. We found General Sheridan there ahead of us, and mighty glad was I to see that brave and able commander once more. Sheridan was accompanied by General Frye and General Forsythe, and all were en route for the Red Cloud Agency, near the center of the Sioux trouble, which was then reaching really alarming proportions. The command was to remain at Laramie for a few days; so, at General Sheridan's request, I accompanied him on his journey. We were able to accomplish little in the way of peace overtures.

The Indians had lately committed many serious depredations along the Black Hills trail. Gold had been discovered there in many new places, and the miners, many of them tenderfoots, and unused to the ways of the red man, had come into frequent conflict with their new neighbors. Massacres, some of them very flagrant, had resulted and most of the treaties our Government had made with the Indians had been ruthlessly broken.

On my return from the agency, the Fifth Cavalry was sent out to scout the country between there and the Black Hills. We operated along the south fork of the Cheyenne and about the foot of the Black Hills for two weeks, and had several small engagements with roving bands of Indians during that time.

All these bands were ugly and belligerent, and it was plain from the spirit they showed that there had been a general understanding among all the redskins thereabout that the time had come to drive the white man from the country.

Brevet-General Wesley Merritt, who had lately received his promotion to the colonelcy of the Fifth Cavalry, now took command of the regiment. I regretted that the command had been taken from General Carr. I was fond of him personally, and it was under him that the regiment made its fine reputation as a fighting organization. I soon became well acquainted with General Merritt, however, and found him to be a brave man and an excellent officer.

The regiment did continuous and hard scouting. We soon believed we had driven all the hostile Indians out of that part of the country. In fact, we were starting back to Fort Laramie, regarding the business at hand as finished, when a scout arrived at our camp and reported the massacre of General Custer and his whole force on the Little Big Horn.

This massacre occurred June 25, 1876, and its details are known, or ought to be known, by every schoolboy. Custer was a brave, dashing, headlong soldier, whose only fault was recklessness.

He had been warned many times never to expose a

small command to a superior force of Indians, and never to underestimate the ability and generalship of the Sioux. He had unbounded confidence, however, in himself and his men, and I believe that not until he was struck down did he ever doubt that he would be able to cut his way out of the wall of warriors about him and turn defeat into a glorious and conspicuous victory.

The news of the massacre, which was the most terrible that ever overtook a command of our soldiers, was a profound shock to all of us. We knew at once that we would all have work to do, and settled grimly into the preparations for it.

Colonel Stanton, who was with the Fifth Cavalry on this scout, had been sent to the Red Cloud Agency two days before. That night a message came from him that eight hundred warriors had left the agency to join Sitting Bull on the Little Big Horn. Notwithstanding instructions to proceed immediately by way of Fort Fetterman to join Crook, General Merritt took the responsibility of endeavoring to intercept the Cheyennes and thereby performed a very important service.

For this job the general selected five hundred men and horses. In two hours we were making a forced march back to War Bonnet Creek. Our intention was to reach the Indian trail running to the north across this watercourse before the Cheyennes could get there. We arrived the next night.

At daylight the next morning, July 17, I proceeded ahead on a scout. I found that the Indians had not yet crossed the creek. On my way back to the command I discovered a large party of Indians. I got close enough to observe them, and they proved to be Cheyennes, coming from the south.

With this information. I hurried back to report.

The cavalrymen were ordered to mount their horses quietly

and remain out of sight, while General Merritt, accompanied by two or three aides and myself, went on a little tour of observation to a neighboring hill. From the summit of this we saw the Indians approaching almost directly toward us. As we stood watching, fifteen or twenty of them wheeled and dashed off to the west, from which direction we had come the night before.

Searching the country to see what it was which had caused this unexpected maneuver, we observed two mounted soldiers approaching us on the trail. Obviously they were bearing dispatches from the command of General Merritt.

It was clear that the Indians who had left their main body were intent on intercepting and murdering these two men. General Merritt greatly feared that they would accomplish this purpose. How to aid them was a problem. If soldiers were sent to their assistance, the Indians would observe the rescuers, and come to the right conclusion that a body of troops was lying in wait for them. This of course would turn them back, and the object of our expedition would be defeated.

The commander asked me if I had any suggestions.

"General," I replied, "why not wait until the scouts get a little nearer? When they are about to charge on the two men, I will take fifteen soldiers, dash down and cut them off from their main body. That will prevent them from going back to report, and the others will fall into our trap."

The general at once saw the possibilities of the scheme. "If you can do that, Cody, go ahead," he said.

I at once rushed back to the command and jumped on my horse.

With fifteen of the best men I could pick in a hurry I returned to the point of observation. I placed myself and my men at the order of General Merritt, and asked him to give me the word at the proper time.

He was diligently studying the country before him with his field-glasses. When he thought the Indians were as close to the unsuspecting scouts as was safe, he sang out:

"Go on now, Cody, and be quick about it. They are going to charge on the couriers."

The two soldiers were not more than a hundred yards from us. The Indians, now making ready to swoop down, were a hundred yards further on.

We tore over the bluffs and advanced at a gallop. They saw us and gave battle. A running fight lasted for several minutes, during which we drove them back a fairly safe distance and killed three of their number.

The main body of the Cheyennes had now come into plain sight, and the men who escaped from us rode back toward it. The main force halted when its leaders beheld the skirmish, and seemed for a time at a loss as to what was best to do.

We turned toward General Merritt, and when we had made about half the distance the Indians we had been chasing suddenly turned toward us and another lively skirmish took place.

One of the Indians, who was elaborately decorated with all the ornaments usually worn by a great chief when he engaged in a fight, saw me and sang out:

"I know you, Pa-ho-has-ka! Come and fight with me!"

The name he used was one by which I had long been known by the Indians. It meant Long-Yellow-Hair.

The chief was riding his horse to and fro in front of his men, in order to banter me. I concluded to accept his challenge.

I turned and galloped toward him for fifty yards, and he rode toward me about the same distance. Both of us rode at full speed. When we were only thirty yards apart I raised my rifle and fired. His horse dropped dead under him, and he rolled over on the ground to clear himself of the carcass.

Almost at the same instant my own horse stepped into a hole and fell heavily. The fall hurt me but little, and almost instantly I was on my feet. This was no time to lie down and nurse slight injuries. The chief and I were now both on our feet, not twenty paces apart. We fired at each other at the same instant. My usual luck held. His bullet whizzed harmlessly past my head, while mine struck him full in the breast.

He reeled and fell, but I took no chances. He had barely touched the ground, when I was upon him, knife in hand, and to make sure of him drove the steel into his heart.

This whole affair, from beginning to end, occupied but little time. The Indians, seeing that I was a little distance from my pony, now came charging down upon me from the hill, in the hope of cutting me off.

General Merritt had witnessed the duel, and, realizing the danger I was in, ordered Colonel Mason with Company K to hurry to my rescue. This order came none too soon. Had it been given one minute later two hundred Indians would have been upon me, and this present narration would have had to be made by some one else. As the soldiers came up I swung the war-bonnet high in the air and shouted: "The first scalp for Custer!"

It was by this time clear to General Merritt that he could not ambush the Indians. So he ordered a general charge. For a time they made a stubborn resistance, but no eight hundred Indians, or twice that number, for that matter, could make a successful stand against such veteran and fearless fighters as the

Fifth Cavalry. They soon came to that conclusion themselves and began a running retreat for the Red Cloud Agency.

For thirty-five miles, over the roughest kind of ground, we drove them before us. Soon they were forced to abandon their spare horses and all the equipment they had brought along. Despite the imminent risk of encountering thousands of other Indians at the Agency, we drove our late adversaries directly into it. No one in our command had any assurance that the Indians gathered there had not gone on the warpath, but little difference that made to us. The Fifth Cavalry, on the warpath itself, would stop at nothing. It was dark when we entered the reservation. All about us we could see the huddling forms of Indians—thousands of them—enough, in fact, to have consummated another Custer massacre. But they showed no disposition to fight.

While at the Agency I learned that the Indian I had killed in the morning was none other than Yellow Hand, a son of old Cut Nose, who was a leading chief of the Cheyennes. The old man learned from the members of Yellow Hand's party that I had killed his son, and sent a white interpreter to me offering four mules in exchange for the young chief's war-bonnet. This request I was obliged to refuse, as I wanted it as a trophy of the first expedition to avenge the death of Custer and his men.

The next morning we started to join the command of General Crook, which was encamped at the foot of Cloud Peak in the Big Horn Mountains. They had decided to await the arrival of the Fifth Cavalry before proceeding against the Sioux, who were somewhere near the head of the Big Horn River, in a country that was as nearly inaccessible as any of the Western fastnesses. By making rapid marches we reached Crook's camp on Goose Creek about the third of August.

At this camp I met many of my old friends, among them

being Colonel Royal, who had just received his promotion to a lieutenant-colonelcy. Royal introduced me to General Crook, whom I had never met before, but with whose reputation as an Indian fighter I was of course familiar, as was everybody in the West. The general's chief guide was Frank Grouard, a half- breed, who had lived six years with Sitting Bull himself, and who was thoroughly familiar with the Sioux and their country.

After one day in camp the whole command pulled out for Tongue River, leaving the wagons behind. Our supplies were carried by a big pack-train. Down the Tongue we marched for two days of hard going, thence westerly to the Rosebud River. Here we struck the main Indian trail leading down- stream. From the size of this trail, which was not more than four days old, we estimated that at least seven thousand Indians, one of the biggest Indian armies ever gathered together, must have gone that way. It was here that we were overtaken by Captain Jack Crawford, widely known East and West as "The Poet Scout." Crawford had just heard of the Custer massacre, and had written a very creditable poem upon receipt of the news. His pen was always ready, and he made many epics of the West, many of which are still popular throughout the country.

Jack was a tenderfoot at that time, having lately come to that country. But he had abundant pluck and courage. He had just brought dispatches to Crook from Fort Fetterman, riding more than three hundred miles through a country literally alive with hostile Indians. These dispatches notified Crook that General Terry was to operate with a large command south of the Yellowstone, and that the two commands would probably consolidate somewhere on the Rosebud. On learning that I was with Crook, Crawford at once hunted me up, and gave me a letter from General Sheridan, announcing his appointment as a scout. He also informed me that he had brought me a present from General Jones, of Cheyenne.

"What kind of a present?" I inquired, seeing no indication of any package about Jack.

"A bottle of whisky!" he almost shouted.

I clapped my hand over his mouth. News that whisky was in the camp was likely to cause a raid by a large number of very dry scouts and soldier men. Only when Jack and I had assured ourselves that we were absolutely alone did I dare dip into his saddle pockets and pull forth the treasure. I will say in passing that I don't believe there is another scout in the West that would have brought a full bottle of whisky three hundred miles. But Jack was "bone dry." As Crawford refused to join me, and I was never a lone drinker, I invited General Carr over to sample the bottle. We were just about to have a little drink for two when into camp rode young Lathrop, the reporter for the Associated Press to whom we had given the name of Death Rattler. Death Rattler appeared to have scented the whisky from afar, for he had no visible errand with us. We were glad to have him, however, as he was a good fellow, and certainly knew how to appreciate a drink.

For two or three days the command pushed on, but we did not seem to gain much on the Indians. They apparently knew exactly where we were and how fast we were going, and they moved just as fast as we did.

On the fourth day of our pursuit I rode about ten miles ahead of the command till I came to a hill which gave a fine view of the surrounding country. Mounting this, I searched the hills with my field-glasses. Soon I saw a great column of smoke rising about ten miles down the creek. As this cloud drifted aside in the keen wind, I could see a column of men marching beneath it. These I at first believed to be the Indians we were after, but closer study revealed them as General Terry's soldiers. I forthwith dispatched a scout who was with me to take this news to Crook. But he had no more than gone when I discovered a band of Indians on the opposite side of the creek and another party of them directly in front of me.

For a few minutes I fancied that I had made a mistake, and that the men I had seen under the dust were really Indians after all.

But very shortly I saw a body of soldiers forming a skirmish line. Then I knew that Terry's men were there, and that the Indians I had seen were Terry's scouts. These Indians had mistaken me for an Indian, and, believing that I was the leader of a big party, shouted excitedly: "The Sioux are coming." That is why the general threw out the skirmish line I had observed.

General Terry, on coming into the Post, ordered the Seventh Cavalry to form a line of battle across the Rosebud; he also brought up his artillery and had the guns unlimbered for action, doubtless dreading another Custer massacre.

These maneuvers I witnessed from my hill with considerable amusement, thinking the command must be badly frightened. After I had enjoyed the situation to my heart's content I galloped toward the skirmish line, waving my hat. When I was within a hundred yards of the troops, Colonel Wier of the Seventh Cavalry rode out to meet me. He recognized me at once, and convoyed me inside the line, shouting to the soldiers:

"Boys, here's Buffalo Bill!" Thereupon three rousing cheers ran all the way down the line.

Colonel Wier presented me to General Terry. The latter questioned me closely and was glad to learn that the alarm had been a false one. I found that I was not entitled alone to the credit of having frightened the whole Seventh Cavalry. The Indian scouts had also seen far behind me the dust raised by Crook's troops, and were fully satisfied that a very large force of Sioux was in the vicinity and moving to the attack.

At General Terry's request I accompanied him as he rode forward to meet Crook. That night both commands went into camp on the Rosebud. General Terry had his wagon-train with him, so the camp had everything to make life as comfortable as it can be on an Indian trail.

The officers had large wall-tents, with portable beds to stow inside them, and there were large hospital tents to be used as dining-rooms. Terry's camp looked very comfortable and homelike. It presented a sharp contrast to the camp of Crook, who had for his headquarters only one small fly-tent, and whose cooking utensils consisted of a quart cup in which he brewed his own coffee, and a sharp stick on which he broiled his bacon. When I compared these two camps I concluded that Crook was a real Indian fighter. He had plainly learned that to follow Indians a soldier must not be hampered by any great weight of luggage or equipment.

That evening General Terry ordered General Miles, with the Fifth Infantry, to return by a forced march to the Yellowstone, and to proceed by steamboat down that stream to the mouth of the Powder River, where the Indians could be intercepted in case they made an attempt to cross the stream. The regiment made a forced march that night of thirty-five miles, which was splendid traveling for an infantry regiment through a mountainous country.

Generals Crook and Terry spent the evening and the next day in council. The following morning both commands moved out on the Indian trail. Although Terry was the senior officer, he did not assume command of both expeditions. Crook was left in command of his own troops, though the two forces operated together. We crossed the Tongue River and moved on to the Powder, proceeding down that stream to a point twenty miles from its junction with the Yellowstone. There the Indian trail turned to the southeast, in the direction of the Black Hills.

The two commands were now nearly out of supplies. The trail was abandoned, and the troops kept on down the Powder River to its confluence with the Yellowstone. There we remained for several days.

General Nelson A. Miles, who was at the head of the Fifth Infantry, and who had been scouting in the vicinity, reported that no Indians had as yet crossed the Yellowstone. Several steamboats soon arrived with large quantities of supplies, and the soldiers, who had been a little too close to famine to please them, were once more provided with full stomachs on which they could fight comfortably, should the need for fighting arise.

One evening while we were in camp on the Yellowstone at the mouth of the Powder River I was informed that Louis Richard, a half-breed scout, and myself, had been selected to accompany General Miles on a reconnaisance. We were to take the steamer Far West down the Yellowstone as far as Glendive Creek. We were to ride in the pilot-house and keep a sharp look-out for Indians on both banks of the river. The idea of scouting from a steamboat was to me an altogether novel one, and I was immensely pleased at the prospect.

At daylight the next morning we reported on the steamer to General Miles, who had with him four or five companies of his regiment. We were somewhat surprised when he asked us why we had not brought our horses. We were at a loss to see how we could employ horses in the pilothouse of a river steamboat. He said that we might need them before we got back, so we sent for them and had them brought on board.

In a few minutes we were looking down the river, the swift current enabling the little steamer to make a speed of twenty miles an hour.

The commander of the Far West was Captain Grant March, a fine chap of whom I had often heard. For many years he was one of the most famous swift-water river captains in the country. It was on his steamer that the wounded from the battle of the Little Big Horn had been transported to Fort Abraham Lincoln, on the Missouri River. On that trip he made the fastest steamboat time on record. He was an excellent pilot, and handled his boat in those swift and dangerous waters with remarkable dexterity.

With Richard and me at our station in the pilothouse the little steamer went flying down-stream past islands, around bends, and over sandbars at a rate that was exhilarating, but sometimes a little disquieting to men who had done most of their navigating on the deck of a Western pony. Presently, far away inland, I thought I could see horses grazing, and reported this belief to General Miles. The general pointed out a large tree on the bank, and asked the captain if he could land the boat there.

"I can not only land her there; I can make her climb the tree if you think it would be any use," returned March.

He brought the boat skillfully alongside the tree, and let it go at that, as the general could see no particular advantage in sending the steamboat up the tree.

Richard and I were ordered to take our horses and push out as rapidly as possible to see if there were any Indians in the vicinity. Meanwhile, General Miles kept his soldiers in readiness to march instantly if we reported any work for them to do.

As we rode off, Captain March, sang out:

"Boys, if there was only a heavy dew on the grass, I could send the old craft right along after you."

It was a false alarm, however. The objects I had seen proved to be Indian graves, with only good Indians in them. On arriving at Glendive Creek we found that Colonel Rice and his company of the Fifth Infantry which had been sent on ahead by General Miles had built a good little fort with their trowel bayonets. Colonel Rice was the inventor of this weapon, and it proved very useful in Indian warfare. It is just as deadly in a charge as the regular bayonet, and can also be used almost as effectively as a shovel for digging rifle-pits and throwing up intrenchments.

The Far West was to remain at Glendive overnight. General Miles wanted a scout to go at once with messages for General Terry, and I was selected for the job. That night I rode seventy-five miles through the Bad Lands of the Yellowstone. I reached General Terry's camp the next morning, after having nearly broken my neck a dozen times or more.

Anyone who has seen that country in the daytime knows that it is not exactly the kind of a place one would pick out for pleasure riding. Imagine riding at night, over such a country, filled with almost every imaginable obstacle to travel, and without any real roads, and you can understand the sort of a ride I had that night. I was mighty glad to see the dawn break, and to be able to pick my way a little more securely, although I could not increase the pace at which I had driven my horse through the long, dark night.

There was no present prospect of carrying this out, however. After I had taken lunch, General Terry asked me if I would carry some dispatches to General Whistler, and I replied that I would be glad to do so. Captain Smith, Terry's aide-de-camp, offered me his horse, and I was glad to accept the animal, as my own was pretty well spent. He proved to be a fine mount. I rode him forty miles that night in four hours, reaching General Whistler's steamboat at four in the morning. When Whistler had read the dispatches I handed him he said:

"Cody, I want to send information to General Terry concerning the Indians that have been skirmishing around here all day. I have been trying to induce some member in my command to carry them, but no one wants to go."

"Get your dispatches ready, general," I replied, "and I'll take them."

He went into his quarters and came out presently with a package, which he handed me. I mounted the same horse which had brought me, and at eight o'clock that evening reached Terry's headquarters, just as his force was about to march.

As soon as Terry had read the dispatches he halted his command, which was already under way. Then he rode on ahead to overtake General Crook, with whom he held a council. At General Terry's urgent request I accompanied him on a scout for Dry Fork, on the Missouri. We marched three days, a little to the east of north. When we reached the buffalo range we discovered some fresh Indian signs. The redskins had been killing buffalo, and the evidences of their work were very plain. Terry now called on me to carry dispatches to Colonel Rice, who was still encamped at the mouth of Glendive Creek on the Yellowstone. This was about eighty miles distant.

Night had set in with a storm. A drizzling rain was falling, which made the going slippery, and made the blackness of the Western Plains still blacker. I was entirely unacquainted with the section of the country through which I was to ride. I therefore traveled all night and remained in seclusion in the daytime. I had too many plans for the future to risk a shot from a hostile redskin who might be hunting white men along my way.

At daylight I unsaddled my mount and made a hearty breakfast of bacon and hardtack. Then I lighted my pipe, and, making a pillow of my saddle, lay down to rest.

The smoke and the fatigue of the night's journey soon made me drowsy, and before I knew it I was fast asleep. Suddenly I was awakened by a loud rumbling noise. I seized my gun instantly, and sprang toward my horse, which I had picketed in a hidden spot in the brush near by where he would be out of sight of any passing Indians.

Climbing a steep hill, I looked cautiously over the country from which the noise appeared to come. There before me was a great herd of buffalo, moving at full gallop. Twenty Indians were behind it, riding hard and firing into the herd as they rode. Others near by were cutting up the carcasses of the animals that had already been killed.

I saddled my horse and tied him near me. Then I crawled on my stomach to the summit of the hill, and for two hours I lay there watching the progress of the chase.

When the Indians had killed all the buffalo they wanted they rode off in the direction whence they had come. This happened to be the way that I hoped to go on my own expedition. I made up my mind that their camp was located somewhere between me and Glendive Creek. I was not at all eager to have any communication with these gentlemen. Therefore, when I resumed my journey at nightfall, I made a wide detour around the place where I believed their camp would be. I avoided it successfully, reaching Colonel Rice's camp just after daybreak.

The colonel had been fighting Indians almost every day since he encamped at this point. He was anxious that Terry should know of this so that reënforcements might be sent, and the country cleared of the redskins. Of course it fell to my lot to carry this word back to Terry.

I undertook the mission willingly enough, for by this time I was pretty well used to night riding through a country beset with perils, and rather enjoyed it.

The strain of my recent rides had told on me, but the excitement bore me up. Indeed, when a man is engaged in work of this kind, the exhilaration is such that he forgets all about the wear and tear on his system, and not until all danger is over and he is safely resting in camp does he begin to feel what he has been through. Then a good long sleep usually puts him all right again.

Many and many a time I have driven myself beyond what I believed was the point of physical endurance, only to find that I was ready for still further effort if the need should arise. The fact that I continued in rugged health during all the time I was on the Plains, and have had little illness throughout my life, seems to prove that living and working outdoors, despite its hardships, is far better for a man than any sedentary occupation can possibly be.

I started back to overhaul General Terry, and on the third day out I found him at the head of Deer Creek. He was on his way to Colonel Rice's camp. He was headed in the right direction, but bearing too far east. He asked me to guide his command in the right course, which I did. On arriving at Glendive I bade good-by to the general and his officers and took passage on the Far West, which was on her way down the Missouri. At Bismarck I left the steamer, and proceeded by rail to Rochester, New York.

It has been a great pleasure to me to meet and know and serve with such men as Crook and Miles. I had served long enough on the Plains to know Indian fighters when I saw them, and I cannot close this chapter without a tribute to both of these men.

Miles had come to the West as a young man with a brilliant war record, having risen to a major-general of volunteers at the age, I think, of 26 or 27.

He took naturally to Indian fighting. He quickly divested himself of all the tactics that were useless in this particular kind of warfare, and learned as much about the Indians as any man ever knew.

Years later, when I was giving my Wild West Show in Madison Square Garden, General Miles visited it as my guest.

The Indians came crowding around him, and followed him wherever he went, although other army officers of high reputation accompanied him on the visit.

This Indian escort at last proved to be almost embarrassing, for the general could not go to any part of the Garden without four or five of the braves silently dogging his footsteps and drinking in his every word.

When this was called to my attention I called one of the old men aside and asked him why he and his brothers followed Miles so eagerly.

"Heap big chief!" was the reply. "Him lickum Injun chiefs. Him biggest White Chief. Heap likum." Which was really a very high tribute, as Indians are not given to extravagant praise.

When we have met from time to time General Miles has been kind enough to speak well of me and the work I have done on the Plains. I am very glad to have this opportunity of returning the compliment.

Crook was a man who lived and fought without any ostentation, but who had high courage and used rare judgment. The fact that he had command of the forces in the West had much to do with their successes in subduing the hostile red man.

Indeed, had not our army taught the Indians that it was never safe, and usually extremely dangerous, to go on the warpath against the Big White Chief, organizations might have been formed which would have played sad havoc with our growing Western civilization.

I am and always have been a friend of the Indian. I have always sympathized with him in his struggle to hold the country that was his by right of birth.

But I have always held that in such a country as America the march of civilization was inevitable, and that sooner or later the men who lived in roving tribes, making no real use of the resources of the country, would be compelled to give way before the men who tilled the soil and used the lands as the Creator intended they should be used.

In my dealings with the Indians we always understood each other. In a fight we did our best to kill each other. In times of peace we were friends. I could always do more with the Indians than most white men, and I think my success in getting so many of them to travel with my organization was because I understood them and they understood me.

Shrewd as were the generals who conducted the fight against the Indians, I believe they could have done little without the services of the men who all over the West served them in the capacity of scouts.

The adventures of small scouting parties were at times even more thrilling than the battles between the Indians and the troops.

Among the ablest of the scouts I worked with in the West were Frank Grouard and Baptiste Pourier. At one time in his childhood Grouard was to all intents and purposes a Sioux

Indian. He lived with the tribe, hunted and fought with them, and wore the breech-clout as his only summer garment.

He met some hunters and trappers while living this life. Their language recalled his childhood, and he presently deserted his red-skinned friends and came back to his own race.

His knowledge of the tongues of the Sioux, Cheyenne, and Crow Indians and his marvelous proficiency in the universal sign language made him an extremely desirable acquisition to the service.

Grouard and "Big Bat" (Baptiste Pourier) were the two scouts that guided Lieutenant Sibley, a young officer of experience and ability, on a scout with about thirty officers and John Finnerty of the ChicagoTimes, a newspaper man who was known all over the West.

At eight o'clock at night they left their halting-place, Big Goose Creek, and in the silent moonlight made a phantom promenade toward the Little Big Horn.

Presently they made out the presence of a war party ahead of them, and one of the scouts of this outfit began riding around in a circle, which meant that the enemy had been discovered.

There were too many Indians to fight in the open, so Grouard led the soldiers to a deep thicket where there were plenty of logs and fallen timber out of which to make breastworks.

The Indians repeatedly circled around them and often charged, but the white men, facing a massacre like that of Custer's men, steadily held them at bay by accurate shooting.

Soon red reënforcements began to arrive. The Indians, feeling that they had now a sufficient advantage, attempted another charge, as the result of which they lost White Antelope, one of the bravest of their chiefs.

This dampened their ardor, but they kept up an incessant firing that rattled against the log breastworks like hailstones.

Fearing that the Indians would soon start a fire and burn them out, Sibley ordered a retreat. The two scouts were left behind to keep up a desultory fire after night had fallen, in order to make the Indians think the party was still in its breastworks. Then the other men in single file struggled up the precipitous sides of the mountain above them, marching, stumbling, climbing, and falling according to the character of the ground they passed over.

The men left behind finally followed on. The temperature fell below zero, and the night was one of suffering and horror. At last they gained a point in the mountains about twenty-five miles distant from Crook's command.

Halting in a sheltered cave, they got a little sleep and started out just in time to escape observation by a large war-party which was scouting in their direction.

At night the jaded party, more dead than alive, forded Tongue River up to their armpits. Two were so exhausted that it was not considered advisable to permit them to plunge into the icy stream, and they were left on the bank till help could be sent to them.

Those that got across dragged themselves over the trail to Crook's camp. The rocks had broken their boots, and with bleeding feet and many a bullet wound they managed to get within sight of the camp, where two men of the Second Cavalry found them and brought them in.

Sibley's men threw themselves on the ground, too exhausted to go another step.

Hot food was brought them, and they soon were strong enough to go to Camp Cloud Peak, to receive the hospitality and sympathy of their comrades. The two men who had been left behind were brought in and cared for.

This expedition was one of the most perilous in the history of the Plains, and the fact that there were any survivors is due to the skill, coolness, and courage of the two scouts, Grouard and Pourier.

❐

# Chapter–10.

My work on the Plains brought me many friends, among them being some of the truest and staunchest that any man ever had. You who live your lives in cities or among peaceful ways cannot always tell whether your friends are the kind who would go through fire for you. But on the Plains one's friends have an opportunity to prove their mettle. And I found out that most of mine would as cheerfully risk their lives for me as they would give me a light for my pipe when I asked it.

Such a friend was old "Buffalo Chips," who certainly deserves a place in these memoirs of mine.

One morning while I was sitting on my porch at North Platte, playing with my children, I saw a man limping on crutches from the direction of the Post hospital. He was a middle-aged man, but had long, flowing white hair, and the most deeply-pitted face I have ever beheld.

Noticing that he seemed confused and in trouble, I sent the children out to bring him to me. He came up haltingly, and in response to my questioning told me that he had been rejected by the hospital because he had been a Confederate soldier and it was against their rules to accept any but Union veterans.

I turned the stranger over to my sister, who prepared a meal for him while I went over to the adjutant's office to see what could be done. I met General Emory in the adjutant's office, and on my promise to pay the ex-Confederate's bills, he gave me an order admitting him to the hospital. Soon my new protégé, who said his name was Jim White, was duly installed, and receiving the treatment of which he stood in sore need.

In a few weeks he had nearly recovered from the wound in his leg which had necessitated the use of his crutches. Every day he came to my house to play with the children and to care for my horses, a service for which he gruffly refused to accept any pay.

Now and then he would borrow one of my rifles for a little practice. I soon discovered that he was a splendid shot, as well as an unusually fine horseman. My surprise at these accomplishments was somewhat lessened when he told me that he had spent his four years' war service as one of General J.E.B. Stuart's scouts. Stuart had no other kind of men in his command.

For years, wherever I went, no matter how dangerous the errand, my new friend went along. The first time he followed me I still remember vividly. I had left the Post on a five days' scout, and was particularly anxious that no one should know the direction I was to take.

When I was four or five miles from the Post I looked back and saw a solitary horseman riding in my direction about a mile in my rear. When I stopped he stopped. I rode on for a little way and looked around again. He was exactly the same distance behind me, and pulled his horse up when I halted. This maneuver I repeated several times, always with the same result.

Considerably disquieted by this mysterious pursuit, I decided to discover the reason for it. I whipped up my horse and when I had put a sandhill between myself and the man behind I made a quick detour through a ravine, and came up in his rear. Then I boldly rode up till I came abreast of him.

He swung around when he heard me coming, and blushed like a girl when he saw how I had tricked him.

"Look here, White," I demanded, "what the devil are you following me in this way for?"

"Mrs. Cody said I could follow you if I wanted to," he said, "and, well, I just followed you, that's all."

That was all he would say. But I knew that he had come along to keep me from getting hurt if I was attacked, and would rather die than admit his real reason. So I told him to come along, and come along he did.

There was no need for his services on that occasion, but a little later he put me in debt to him for my life. He and I rode together into a border town, where there were a few gentlemen in the horse-stealing business who had reason to wish me moved along to some other sphere. I left White to look after the horses as we reached the town, and went into a hotel to get a nip, for which I felt a very great need. White noticed a couple of rough-looking chaps behind the barn as he put the horses away and quietly slipped to a window where he could overhear their conversation.

"We'll go in while he is taking a drink," one of them was saying, "and shoot him from behind. He'll never have a chance."

Without a word to me, White hurried into the hotel and got behind the door. Presently the two men entered, both with drawn revolvers. But before they could raise them White covered them with his own weapon and commanded them sternly to throw up their hands, an order with which they instantly complied after one look at his face.

I wheeled at the order, and recognized his two captives as

the men I was looking for, a pair of horse-thieves and murderers whom I had been sent to apprehend. My revolvers were put into instant requisition, and I kept them covered while White removed the guns with which they had expected to put me out of their way.

With White's help I conducted these gentlemen forty miles back to the sheriff's office, and they walked every step of the way. Each of them got ten years in the penitentiary as soon as they could be tried. They either forgave me or forgot me when they got out, for I never heard of either of them again.

In the campaign of 1876 I secured employment for White as a scout. He was with me when Terry and Crook's commands separated on the Yellowstone. By this time he had come to copy my gait, my dress, my speech, and even my fashion of wearing my hair down on my shoulders, though mine at that time was brown, and his was white as the driven snow.

We were making a raid on an Indian village, which was peopled with very lively and very belligerent savages. I had given White an old red-lined coat, one which I had worn conspicuously in a number of battles, and which the Indians had marked as a special target on that account.

A party of Indians had been driven from among the lodges into a narrow gorge, and some of the soldiers, among them Captain Charles King, had gone after them. As they were proceeding cautiously, keeping tinder cover as much as possible, King observed White creeping along the opposite bluff, rifle in hand, looking for a chance at the savages huddled below, and hoping to distract their fire so they would do as little damage as possible to the soldiers who were closing in on them.

White crawled along on all-fours till he reached a stunted tree on the brim of the ravine. There he halted, brought his rifle to his shoulder in readiness to aim and raised himself slowly to his feet. He was about to fire, when one of the Indians in the hole below spotted the red-lined coat. There was a crack, a puff of smoke, and White toppled over, with a bullet through his heart.

The coat had caught the attention of the savages, and thus I had been the innocent means of my friend's death; for, with the soldiers pressing them so hard, it is not likely that any of the warriors would have wasted a shot had they not thought they were getting Pa-ho-has-ka. For a long time the Indians believed that I would be a menace to them no more. But they discovered their mistake later, and I sent a good many of them to the Happy Hunting- Grounds as a sort of tribute to my friend.

Poor old White! A more faithful man never took a trail, nor a braver. He was a credit to me, and to the name which General Sheridan had first given him in derision, but which afterward became an honor, the name of "Buffalo Chips."

When Terry and Crook's commands joined on the Yellowstone both commands went into camp together and guards were placed to prevent surprise. The scene was typical of the Old West, but it would astonish anyone whose whole idea of warfare has been gained by a visit to a modern military post or training camp, or the vast camps where the reserve forces are drilled and equipped for the great European war.

Generals Crook, Merritt, and Carr were in rough hunting rigs, utterly without any mark of their rank. Deerskin, buckskin, corduroy, canvas, and rags indiscriminately covered the rest of the command, so that unless you knew the men it was totally impossible to distinguish between officers and enlisted men. However, every one in the commands knew every one else, and there was no confusion.

A great part of that night was spent in swapping stories of

recent experiences. All of them were thrilling, even to veteran campaigners fresh from the trail. There was no need of drawing the long bow in those days. The truth was plenty exciting enough to suit the most exacting, and we sat about like schoolboys, drinking in each other's tales, and telling our own in exchange.

A story of a personal adventure and a hairbreadth escape in which Lieutenant De Rudio figured was so typical of the fighting days of the West that I want my readers to know it. I shall tell it, as nearly as I can, just as it came to me around the flickering fire in that picturesque border camp.

De Rudio had just returned from his adventure, and he told it to us between puffs of his pipe so realistically that I caught several of my old friends of the Plains peering about into the darkness as if to make sure that no lurking redskins were creeping up on them.

In the fight of a few days before De Rudio was guarding a pony crossing with eight men when one of them sang out:

"Lieutenant, get your horse, quick. Reno (the commander of the outfit) is retreating!" No trumpet had sounded, however, and no orders had been given, so the lieutenant hesitated to retire. His men left in a hurry, but he remained, quietly waiting for the call.

Presently, looking behind him, he saw thirty or forty Indians coming full gallop. He wheeled and started to get into safer quarters. As lie did so they cut loose with a volley. He leaned low on his horse as they shot, and the bullets sang harmlessly over his head.

Before him was a fringe of thick underbrush along the river, and into this he forced his unwilling horse. The bullets followed and clipped the twigs about him like scissors. At last he gained the creek, forded, and mounted the bank on the other side. Here, instead of safety, he found hundreds of Indians, all busily shooting at the soldiers, who were retreating discreetly in the face of a greatly superior force. He was entirely cut off from retreat, unless he chose to make a bold dash for his life right through the middle of the Indians. This he was about to do, when a young Indian, who had observed him, sent a shot after him, and his horse fell dead under him, rolling over and over, while he managed to scramble to his feet.

The shot had attracted the attention of all the Indians in that immediate neighborhood, and there were plenty of them there for all offensive purposes. De Rudio jumped down the creek bank and hid in an excavation while a hail of bullets spattered the water ahead of him and raised a dozen little clouds of dust at his feet.

So heavy had this volley been that the Indians decided that the bullets had done their work, and a wild yell broke from them.

Suddenly the yell changed to another sort of outcry, and the firing abruptly ceased. Peering out, De Rudio saw Captain Benteen's column coming up over the hill. He began to hope that his rescue was at hand. But in a few minutes the soldiers disappeared and the Indians all started off after them.

Just beyond the hill was the noise of a lively battle, and he made up his mind that Reno's command had rallied, and that if he could join them he might be saved.

Working his way softly through the brush he was nearing the summit of the slope when he heard his name whispered and saw three of his own company in the brush. Two of them were mounted. The horse of the third had been killed.

The three men remained in the bushes, lying as low as they could and making no sound. Looking out now and then, they could see an old Indian woman going about, taking scalps and mutilating the bodies of the soldiers who had been slain. Most of the warriors were occupied with the battle, but now and then a warrior, suspicious that soldiers were still lurking in the brush, would ride over in their direction and fire a few shots that whistled uncomfortably close to their heads.

Presently the firing on the hill ceased, and hundreds of Indians came slowly back. But they were hard pressed by the soldiers, and the battle was soon resumed, to break out intermittently through the entire night.

In a quiet interval the two soldiers got their horses, and with their companion and De Rudio holding to the animals' tails forded the river and made a détour round the Indians. Several times they passed close to Indians. Once or twice they were fired on and answered the fire, but their luck was with them and they escaped bringing a general attack down upon them.

As they were making their way toward the edge of the clearing they saw directly before them a party of men dressed in the ragged uniforms of American cavalrymen, and all drew deep breaths of relief. Help seemed now at hand. But just as they sprang forward to join their supposed comrades a fiendish yell broke from the horsemen. In another instant the four unfortunates were rushing to cover, with a dozen Indians, all dressed in the clothing taken from dead soldiers, in hot pursuit.

The Indians had been planning a characteristic piece of Sioux strategy. As fast as it could be accomplished they had been stripping the clothing from dead and wounded soldiers and garbing themselves in it with the purpose of deceiving the outposts of Reno's command and surprising the Americans as soon as day broke. Had it not been for the accidental discovery of the ruse by De Rudio's party it might have succeeded only too well.

The lieutenant and his companions managed to get away safely and to find shelter in the woods. But the Indians immediately fired the underbrush and drove them further and further on. Then, just as they had begun to despair of their lives, their pursuers, who had been circling around the tangle of scrub growth, began singing a slow chant and withdrew to the summit of the hill.

There they remained in council a little time and then cantered away single file.

Fearing another trap, the white men remained for weary hours in their hiding-place, but at last were compelled by thirst and hunger to come out.

No Indians were visible, nor did any appear as, worn out and dispirited, they dragged themselves to the camp of the soldiers. In the forty-eight hours since he had been cut off from his command De Rudio had undergone all the horrors of Indian warfare and a hundred times had given himself up for dead.

Bullets had passed many times within a few inches of him. Half a dozen times only a lucky chance had intervened between him and the horrible death that Indians know so well how to inflict. Yet, save for the bruises from his fall off his horse, and the abrasions of the brush through which he had traveled, he had never received a scratch.

❐

# Chapter–11.

Of all the Indians I encountered in my years on the Plains the most resourceful and intelligent, as well as the most dangerous, were the Sioux. They had the courage of dare-devils combined with real strategy. They mastered the white man's tactics as soon as they had an opportunity to observe them. Incidentally they supplied all thinking and observing white commanders with a great deal that was well worth learning in the art of warfare. The Sioux fought to win, and in a desperate encounter were absolutely reckless of life.

But they also fought wisely, and up to the minute of closing in they conserved their own lives with a vast amount of cleverness. The maxim put into words by the old Confederate fox, Forrest: "Get there fastest with the mostest," was always a fighting principle with the Sioux.

They were a strong race of men, the braves tall, with finely shaped heads and handsome features. They had poise and dignity and a great deal of pride, and they seldom forgot either a friend or an enemy.

The greatest of all the Sioux in my time, or in any time for that matter, was that wonderful old fighting man, Sitting Bull, whose life will some day be written by a historian who can really give him his due.

Sitting Bull it was who stirred the Indians to the uprising whose climax was the massacre of the Little Big Horn and the destruction of Custer's command.

For months before this uprising he had been going to and fro among the Sioux and their allies urging a revolt against the encroaching white man. It was easy at that time for the Indians to secure rifles. The Canadian-French traders to the north were only too glad to trade them these weapons for the splendid supplies of furs which the Indians had gathered. Many of these rifles were of excellent construction, and on a number of occasions we discovered to our cost that they outranged the army carbines with which we were equipped.

After the Custer massacre the frontier became decidedly unsafe for Sitting Bull and the chiefs who were associated with him, and he quietly withdrew to Canada, where he was for the time being safe from pursuit.

There he stayed till his followers began leaving him and returning to their reservations in the United States. Soon he had only a remnant of his followers and his immediate family to keep him company. Warily he began negotiating for immunity, and when he was fully assured that if he would use his influence to quiet his people and keep them from the warpath his life would be spared, he consented to return.

He had been lonely and unhappy in Canada. An accomplished orator and a man with a gift of leadership, he had pined for audiences to sway and for men to do his bidding. He felt sure that these would be restored to him once he came back among his people. As to his pledges, I have no doubt that he fully intended to live up to them. He carried in his head all the treaties that had been made between his people and the white men, and could recite their minutest details, together with the dates of their making and the names of the men who had signed for both sides.

But he was a stickler for the rights of his race, and he devoted far more thought to the trend of events than did most of his red brothers.

Here was his case, as he often presented it to me:

"The White Man has taken most of our land. He has paid us nothing for it. He has destroyed or driven away the game that was our meat. In 1868 he arranged to build through the Indians' land a road on which ran iron horses that ate wood and breathed fire and smoke. We agreed. This road was only as wide as a man could stretch his arms. But the White Man had taken from the Indians the land for twenty miles on both sides of it. This land he had sold for money to people in the East. It was taken from the Indians. But the Indians got nothing for it.

"The iron horse brought from the East men and women and children, who took the land from the Indians and drove out the game. They built fires, and the fires spread and burned the prairie grass on which the buffalo fed. Also it destroyed the pasturage for the ponies of the Indians. Soon the friends of the first White Men came and took more land. Then cities arose and always the White Man's lands were extended and the Indians pushed farther and farther away from the country that the Great Father had given them and that had always been theirs.

"When treaties were broken and the Indians trespassed on the rights of the White Man, my chiefs and I were always here to adjust the White Man's wrongs.

"When treaties were broken and the Indians' rights were infringed, no one could find the white chiefs. They were somewhere back toward the rising sun. There was no one to give us justice. New chiefs of the White Men came to supplant the old chiefs. They knew nothing of our wrongs and laughed at us.

"When the Sioux left Minnesota and went beyond the Big Muddy the white chiefs promised them they would never again be disturbed. Then they followed us across the river, and when we asked for lands they gave us each a prairie chicken's flight four ways (a hundred and sixty acres); this they gave us, who once had all the land there was, and whose habit is to roam as far as a horse can carry us and then continue our journey till we have had our fill of wandering."

"We are not as many as the White Man. But we know that this land is our land. And while we live and can fight, we will fight for it. If the White Man does not want us to fight, why does he take our land? If we come and build our lodges on the White Man's land, the White Man drives us away or kills us. Have we not the same right as the White Man?"

The forfeiture of the Black Hills and unwise reduction of rations kept alive the Indian discontent. When, in 1889, Congress passed a law dividing the Sioux reservation into many smaller ones so as to isolate the different tribes of the Dakota nation a treaty was offered them. This provided payment for the ponies captured or destroyed in the war of 1876 and certain other concessions, in return for which the Indians were to cede about half their land, or eleven million acres, which was to be opened up for settlement.

The treaty was submitted to the Indians for a vote. They came in from the woods and the plains to vote on it, and it was carried by a very narrow majority, many of the Indians insisting that they had been coerced by their necessities into casting favorable ballots.

Congress delayed and postponed the fulfillment of the

promised conditions, and the Indian unrest increased as the months went by. Even after the land had been taken over and settled up, Congress did not pass the appropriation that was necessary before the Indians could get their money.

Sitting Bull was appealed to for aid, and once more began employing his powerful gift of oratory in the interest of armed resistance against the white man.

Just at this time a legend whose origin was beyond all power to fathom became current among the red men of the north.

From one tribe to another spread the tidings that a Messiah was to come back to earth to use his miraculous power in the interest of the Indian. The whites were to be driven from the land of the red man. The old days of the West were to be restored. The ranges were to be re-stocked with elk, antelope, deer, and buffalo.

Soon a fever of fanaticism had infected every tribe. Not alone were the Sioux the victims of this amazing delusion, but every tribe on the continent shared in it.

There was to be a universal brotherhood of red men. Old enmities were forgotten. Former foes became fast friends. The Yaquis in Mexico sent out word that they would be ready for the great Armageddon when it came. As far north as Alaska there were ghost dances and barbaric festivities to celebrate the coming restoration of the Indian to the lands of his inheritance.

And as the Indians danced, they talked and sang and thought of war, while their hatred of the white man broke violently forth.

Very much disquieted at the news of what was going on the War Department sent out word to stop the dancing and singing. Stop it! You could as easily have stopped the eruption of Mount Lassen! Among the other beliefs that spread among the Indians was one that all the sick would be healed and be able to go into battle, and that young and old, squaws and braves alike, would be given shirts which would turn the soldiers' bullets like armor-plate.

Every redskin believed that he could not be injured. None of them had any fear of battle, or any suspicions that he could be injured in the course of the great holy war that was to come.

❐

# Chapter–12.

In November, 1890, I was returning from Europe with my Wild West Company. When the New York pilot came aboard he brought a big packet of papers. That was before the days of wireless, and we had had no tidings of what was going on in the world since we had left the other side.

As he came up the ladder he recognized me, and shouted: "Colonel, there's a big Indian war started! I guess you'll be needed out there."

I seized the papers and eagerly read the details of the threatened outbreak. I was not surprised when, on arriving at Quarantine, I was handed a telegram from General Miles.

I was requested to come to Chicago as soon as possible, and to telegraph the time of my arrival. Canceling all New York engagements, I caught the first train for the West, and in thirty-six hours reported to General Miles in his headquarters.

He briefly described to me what had been happening and went over with me the maps of the Western States where the Indians were getting ready for war. He said that it was his understanding that the Bad Lands of North Dakota had been selected as the battle-ground by the Indians, and asked me to give him all the information I possessed about that country and its accessibility for troops.

Miles was about to leave for the Pine Ridge Agency, and take command of the campaign to put down the Indians.

I was thoroughly familiar with the Bad Lands, and spent an hour or more in discussing the coming campaign with the general. We both agreed that the Indians had selected a particularly good country for their uprising, and an especially good season, as in winter, with the hills covered with snow, and blizzards of almost daily occurrence, it would be far harder to hunt them out than in summer, when the troops could travel easily.

Miles said that Sitting Bull had his camp somewhere within forty or fifty miles of the Standing Rock Agency, and was haranguing the Indians thereabout, spreading the Messiah talk and getting them to join him. He asked me if I could go immediately to Standing Rock and Fort Yates, and thence to Sitting Bull's camp.

He knew that I was an old friend of the chief, and he believed that if any one could induce the old fox to abandon his plans for a general war I could. If I could not dissuade him from the warpath the general was of the opinion that I might be able to delay him in taking it, so that troops could be sent into the country in time to prevent a horrible massacre of the defenseless white settlers, who were already in terror of their lives.

I knew that this would be the most dangerous undertaking of my career. I was sure that if I could reach Sitting Bull he would at least listen to me. But in the present inflamed state of the Indian mind it would be next to impossible to get to his camp alive.

Nevertheless I was quite ready to take the risk. I knew what fearful damage could be done by a sudden uprising of fanatical and infuriated Indians, and any danger to me personally was as nothing to the importance of preventing such, a thing, if possible.

Having no standing as an army officer or as a Government agent, it was necessary for me to be supplied with some sort of credentials, in order to secure the assistance I should need on my mission. When I informed General Miles of this he took one of his visiting-cards from a case and wrote the following on the back of it:

To COMMANDING OFFICERS OF UNITED STATES TROOPS:

Furnish Colonel William F. Cody with any assistance or escort that he may ask for.

## Nelson A. Miles

I took the next train for Mandan, N.D., which was the station nearest the Standing Rock Agency. There I hired a livery team and driver for the ride of sixty-five miles to the Agency. I had considerable difficulty in securing a driver, as the report had gone abroad that all the Indians were on the warpath, and few of the settlers cared to risk their scalps on such a venture. But I went higher and higher in my offers, till at last a liveryman figured that a hundred dollars was sufficient reward for the risk, and, hitching up his team, told me to come along.

After an intensely cold drive we reached the Agency, where I hurried into the trader's store to thaw out by his stove. I had hardly arrived before the trader came in and told me that Major McLaughlin, the Indian agent, wanted to see me. News travels very fast in the Indian country, especially in war times. Someone about the Post who had seen me driving in had hurried to headquarters to inform the agent that Buffalo Bill had arrived by way of reënforcements.

As soon as I got my chilled blood into circulation I went to the major's quarters, and informed him of the purpose of my visit. We were old friends, and he was very glad to see me, but he was much concerned on learning what I intended to do.

"That is impossible!" he said. "The Sioux are threatening a great war. At this very moment we do not know when the Indians here at the Agency may rise. We can take care of our own situation, for we have four troops of cavalry here, but we cannot permit you to go to Sitting Bull's camp. Not only would you be killed before you got halfway there, but your presence in the country would precipitate hostilities for which we are not in the least prepared. I'm sorry, Cody, but it can't be done."

More fully to persuade me of the truth of what he said he took me to the quarters of Colonel Brown, the commander of the troops at the Agency, and asked him to talk to me. Brown listened to my statement of what I proposed and shook his head.

"I've heard of you, Cody, and of your nerve, but this is more than even you can do. Sitting Bull's camp is forty miles away, and the country between here and there is swarming with Indians all ready to go on the warpath, and wholly beyond the sway of reason. I cannot permit you to make this attempt."

"Do you hear, Cody?" said McLaughlin. "The only thing for you to do is to stay all night with us and then return to the railroad. Even that will be risky enough, even for you." "But go you must," added Brown. "The Agency is under martial law, and I cannot permit you to remain any longer than tomorrow morning."

There was no arguing with these men. So I resorted to my credentials. Taking General Miles's card from my pocket, I laid it before Colonel Brown.

"What does this mean?" he demanded, and passed the card to McLaughlin. "It looks like orders," said McLaughlin.

"Yes," said Brown, "and I can't disobey them."

Just then Captain Fatchett, an old friend of mine, came into the quarters, and Brown turned me over to him for entertainment until I should formulate my plans for my visit to Sitting Bull. I had never served with the Eighth Cavalry to which the companies at the Post belonged, but I had many friends among the officers, and spent a very pleasant afternoon and evening talking over old times, and getting information about the present situation.

After guard-mount the next morning I told Colonel Brown that I did not think I would require an escort for my visit, as the presence of a number of armed men in the Indian country would be sure to start the trouble it was our purpose to avoid, or to delay as long as possible. The man who had driven me over was anxious to return at once, so I asked for a light spring- wagon and a team of mules.

"Wait an hour or two," said the colonel, "and I'll send the quartermaster to you."

I waited, and he employed the time, as I afterward learned, in telegraphing to General Miles, to the Commissioner of Indian Affairs, to the Secretary of the Interior, and to President Harrison. He informed all of them that I was there, insisting on going to Sitting Bull's camp, and that such an errand would not only result in my death, but would precipitate the outbreak then brewing, and for which he was not at all prepared. He besought all of them to instruct me to return to Mandan.

While he waited for replies to his dispatches I hunted about the camp for someone who knew just where Sitting Bull was located and how to get there. I also wanted a first-class interpreter, as I would have matters to discuss with Sitting Bull beyond his mastery of English or mine of Sioux to express. At last I found a man who agreed to go with me as guide for five hundred dollars, which I promised him without a protest. Then I went over to the post-trader's store and bought all manner of presents which I knew would be acceptable to Sitting Bull, his squaw, and his children.

When I returned to Colonel Brown's quarters he endeavored once more to put me off. But I would not be put off. I informed him that I had explicit orders from General Miles as to my mission, and that if he interfered with me he was violating the orders of his commanding officer and running into very serious trouble.

At last he reluctantly sent for the quartermaster, and ordered him to have a span of good mules hitched to a light spring-wagon.

The wagon was driven to the post-trader's store, where I found my guide and interpreter, and loaded aboard the presents I had bought for the old warrior. With plenty of robes to keep out the intense cold, we started out on our journey, a little apprehensive, but fully determined to go through with it. Five or six miles from the Post we met three men in a wagon driving toward the Agency. They told us that Sitting Bull's camp had been lately moved, and that it was now further down the river. I knew that if the old man was really on the warpath he would be moving up the river, not down, so I felt considerably reassured.

When we had proceeded a few miles further we heard a yell behind us, and, looking back, saw a rider approaching at full speed. This proved to be one of Major McLaughlin's Indian scouts. He bore a telegram reading:

### Colonel William F. Cody, Fort Yates, N.D.

The order for the detention of Sitting Bull has been rescinded. You are hereby ordered to return to Chicago and report to General Miles.

BENJAMIN HARRISON, President.

That ended my mission to Sitting Bull. I still believe I could have got safely through the country, though there were plenty of chances that I would be killed or wounded in the attempt.

I returned to the Post, turned back my presents at a loss to myself, and paid the interpreter fifty dollars for his day's work. He was very glad to have the fifty and a whole skin, for he could not figure how the five hundred would be of much help to him if he had been stretched out on the Plains with an Indian bullet through him.

I was supplied with conveyance back to Mandan by Colonel Brown and took my departure the next morning. Afterward, in Indianapolis, President Harrison informed me that he had allowed himself to be persuaded against my mission in opposition to his own judgment, and said he was very sorry that he had not allowed me to proceed.

It developed afterward that the people who had moved the President to interfere consisted of a party of philanthropists who advanced the argument that my visit would precipitate a war in which Sitting Bull would be killed, and it was to spare the life of this man that I was stopped!

The result of the President's order was that the Ghost Dance War followed very shortly, and with it came the death of Sitting Bull.

I found that General Miles knew exactly why I had been turned back from my trip to Sitting Bull. But he was a soldier, and made no criticism of the order of a superior. General Miles was glad to hear that I had been made a brigadier-general, but he was still more pleased with the fact that I knew so many Indians at the Agency.

"You can get around among them," he said, "and learn their intentions better than any other man I know."

I remained with General Miles until the final surrender of the North American Indians to the United States Government after three hundred years of warfare.

This surrender was made to Miles, then lieutenant-general of the army, and it was eminently fitting that a man who had so ably conducted the fight of the white race against them and had dealt with them so justly and honorably should have received their surrender.

With that event ended one of the most picturesque phases of Western life—Indian fighting. It was with that that I was identified from my youth to my middle age, and in the time I spent on the Plains, Indian warfare reached its greatest severity and its highest development.

❐

# Chapter–13.

In the preceding chapters I have sketched briefly some of the most interesting of my adventures on the Plains. It has been necessary to omit much that I would like to have told. For twenty years my life was one of almost continuous excitement, and to tell the whole story would require many volumes.

It was because of my great interest in the West, and my belief that its development would be assisted by the interest I could awaken in others, that I decided to bring the West to the East through the medium of the Wild West Show. How greatly I was to succeed in this venture I had no idea when it first occurred to me. As I have told you, I had already appeared in a small Western show, and was the first man to bring Indians to the East and exhibit them. But the theater was too small to give any real impression of what Western life was like. Only in an arena where horses could be ridden at full gallop, where lassos could be thrown, and pistols and guns fired without frightening the audience half to death, could such a thing be attempted.

After getting together a remarkable collection of Indians, cowboys, Indian ponies, stage-coach drivers, and other typical denizens of my own country under canvas I found myself almost immediately prosperous.

We showed in the principal cities of the country, and everywhere the novelty of the exhibition drew great crowds. As owner and principal actor in the enterprise I met the leading citizens of the United States socially, and never lost an opportunity to "talk up" the Western country, which I believed to have a wonderful future. I worked hard on the program of the entertainment, taking care to make it realistic in every detail. The wigwam village, the Indian war-dance, the chant of the Great Spirit as it was sung on the Plains, the rise and fall of the famous tribes, were all pictured accurately.

It was not an easy thing to do. Sometimes I had to send men on journeys of more than a hundred miles to get the right kind of war-bonnets, or to make correct copies of the tepees peculiar to a particular tribe. It was my effort, in depicting the West, to depict it as it was. I was much gratified in after years to find that scientists who had carefully studied the Indians, their traditions and habits, gave me credit for making very valuable contributions to the sum of human knowledge of the American native.

The first presentation of my show was given in May, 1883, at Omaha, which I had then chosen as my home. From there we made our first summer tour, visiting practically every important city in the country.

For my grand entrance I made a spectacle which comprised the most picturesque features of Western life. Sioux, Arapahoes, Brulés, and Cheyennes in war-paint and feathers led the van, shrieking their war-whoops and waving the weapons with which they were armed in a manner to inspire both terror and admiration in the tenderfoot audience.

Next came cowboys and soldiers, all clad exactly as they were when engaged in their campaigns against the Indians, and lumbering along in the rear were the old stage-coaches which carried the settlers to the West in the days before the railroad made the journey easy and pleasant.

I am sure the people enjoyed this spectacle, for they flocked in crowds to see it. I know I enjoyed it. There was never a day when, looking back over the red and white men in my cavalcade, I did not know the thrill of the trail, and feel a little sorry that my Western adventures would thereafter have to be lived in spectacles.

Without desiring to dim the glory of any individual I can truthfully state that the expression "rough riders," which afterward became so famous, was my own coinage. As I rode out at the front of my parade I would bow to the audience, circled about on the circus benches, and shout at the top of my voice:

"Ladies and gentlemen, permit me to introduce you to the rough riders of the world!"

For three years we toured the United States with great success. One day an Englishman, whose name I never learned, came to see me after the show.

"That is a wonderful performance," he told me. "Here in America it meets with great appreciation, but you have no idea what a sensation it would be in the Old World, where such things are unheard of."

That set me to thinking. In a few days, after spending hours together considering the matter, I had made up my mind that Europe should have an opportunity to study America as nearly at first-hand as possible through the medium of my entertainment.

Details were soon arranged. In March, 1886, I chartered the steamer State of Nebraska, loaded my Indians, cowboys, horses, and stage-coaches on board, and set sail for another continent.

It was a strange voyage. The Indians had never been to sea

before, and had never dreamed that such an expanse of water existed on the planet. They would stand at the rail, after the first days of seasickness were over, gazing out across the waves, and trying to descry something that looked like land, or a tree, or anything that seemed familiar and like home. Then they would shake their heads disconsolately and go below, to brood and muse and be an extremely unhappy and forlorn lot of savages. The joy that seized them when at last they came in sight of land, and were assured that we did not intend to keep on sailing till we fell over the edge of the earth, was something worth looking at.

At Gravesend we sighted a tug flying the American colors, and when the band on board responded to our cheers with "The Star-Spangled Banner" even the Indians tried to sing. Our band replied with "Yankee Doodle," and as we moved toward port there was more noise on board than I had ever heard in any battle on the Plains.

When the landing was made the members of the party were sent in special coaches to London. Crowds stared at us from every station. The guards on the train were a little afraid of the solemn and surly-looking Indians, but they were a friendly and jovial crowd, and when they had recovered from their own fright at the strange surroundings they were soon on good terms with the Britishers.

Major John M. Burke, who was my lifetime associate in the show business, had made all arrangements for housing the big troupe. We went to work at our leisure with our preparations to astonish the British public, and succeeded beyond our wildest dreams. The big London amphitheater, a third of a mile in circumference, was just the place for such an exhibition.

The artist's brush was employed on lavish scale to reproduce the scenery of the Western Plains. I was busy for many days with preparations, and when our spectacle was finally given it was received with such a burst of enthusiasm as I had never witnessed anywhere.

The show began, after the grand entry, with the hour of dawn on the Plains. Wild animals were scattered about. Within their tents were the Indians sleeping. As the dawn deepened the Indians came out of their tents and went through one of their solemn and impressive war-dances. While this was going on the British audience held its breath. You could have heard a whisper in almost any part of the arena.

Then in came a courier to announce the neighborhood of a hostile tribe. Instantly there was a wild scramble for mounts and weapons. The enemy rushed in, and for ten minutes there was a sham battle which filled the place with noise and confusion. This battle was copied as exactly as it could be copied from one of the scrimmages in which I had taken part in my first days as a scout. Then we gave them a buffalo hunt, in which I had a hand, and did a little fancy shooting. As a finish there was a Wild Western cyclone, and a whole Indian village was blown out of existence for the delectation of the English audience.

The initial performance was given before the Prince and Princess of Wales, afterward King Edward and his Queen, and their suite. At the close of the program the Prince and Princess, at their own request, were introduced to all the leading members of the company, including many of the Indians.

When the cowgirls of the show were presented to the Princess they stepped forward and offered their hands, which were taken and well shaken in true democratic fashion.

Red Shirt, the most important chief in the outfit, was highly pleased when he learned that a princess was to visit him in his camp. He had the Indian gift of oratory, and he replied to her greeting with a long and eloquent speech, in which his gestures, if not his words, expressed plainly the honor he felt in receiving so distinguished a lady. The fact that he referred to Alexandria as a squaw did not seem to mar her enjoyment.

That the Prince was really pleased with the exhibition was shown by the fact that he made an immediate report of it to his mother. Shortly thereafter I received a command from Queen Victoria to appear before her.

This troubled me a good deal—not that I was not more than eager to obey this flattering command, but that I was totally at a loss how to take my show to any of the great residences occupied by Her Majesty.

Finally, after many cautious inquiries, I discovered that she would be willing to visit the show if a special box was prepared for her. This we did to the best of our ability. The box was placed upon a dais covered with crimson velvet and handsomely decorated. When the Queen arrived I met her at the door of the box, with my sombrero in my hand and welcomed her to "the Wild West of America."

One of the first acts in the performance was to carry the flag to the front. This was done by a soldier. Walking around the arena, he offered the Stars and Stripes as an emblem of the friendship of America to all the world. On this occasion he carried the flag directly to the royal box, and dipped it three times before the Queen.

Absolute silence fell over the great throng. Then the Queen rose and saluted the flag with a bow, her suite following her example. There was a wild cheer from everyone in the show, Indians included, and soon all the audience was on its feet, cheering and waving flags and handkerchiefs.

This gave us a fine start and we never put on a better performance. When it was all over Her Majesty sent for me, and paid me many compliments as well as to my country and the West. I found her a most gracious and charming woman, with none of the haughtiness which I had supposed was inseparable from a person of such exalted rank. My subsequent experiences with royalty convinced me that there is more real democracy among the rulers of the countries of Europe than you will find among the petty officials of a village.

It was interesting to watch old Red Shirt when he was presented to the Queen. He clearly felt that this was a ceremony between one ruler and another, and the dignity with which he went through the introduction was wonderful to behold. One would have thought to watch him that most of his life was spent in introductions to kings and queens, and that he was really a little bored with the effort required to go through with them. A second command from the Queen resulted in an exhibition before a number of her royal guests, including the Kings of Saxony, Denmark, and Greece, the Queen of the Belgians, and the Crown Prince of Austria.

The Deadwood coach, one of the features of the show, was of particular interest to my royal guests. This was a coach with a history. It was built in Concord, N.H., and sent by water to San Francisco to run over a route infested with road-agents. A number of times it was held up and robbed. Finally, both driver and passengers were killed and the coach abandoned on the trail. It remained for a long time a derelict, but was afterward brought into San Francisco by an old stage-driver and placed on the Overland trail.

As it worked its way East over the Overland route its old

luck held steadily. Again were driver and passengers massacred; again it was abandoned. At last, when it was "hoodooed" all over the West and no independent driver or company would have anything to do with it I discovered it, bought it, and used it for my show.

One of the incidents of my program, as all who have seen it will remember, was an Indian attack on this coach. The royal visitors wanted a real taste of Western life—insisted on it, in fact, and the Kings of Denmark, Greece, Saxony, and the Crown Prince of Austria climbed to the box with me.

I had secretly instructed the Indians to throw a little real energy into their pursuit of the coach, and they followed my instructions rather more completely than I expected. The coach was surrounded by a demoniac band of shooting and shouting Indians. Blank cartridges were discharged at perilously close proximity to the rulers of four great nations. Looking around to quiet my followers, I saw that the guests of the occasion were a trifle pale, but they were all of them game, and came out of the affair far less scared than were the absolutely terrified members of the royal suites, who sat in their boxes and wrung their hands in wild alarm.

In recognition of this performance the Prince of Wales sent me a souvenir consisting of a feathered crest, outlined in diamonds, with the words "Ich dien" worked in jewels underneath. A note in the Prince's own hand expressed the pleasure of his guests in the entertainment I had provided for them.

After a tour of the principal cities we returned to America, proud of our success, and well rewarded in purse for our effort.

The welcome to America was almost as elaborate as that from

England. I quote from the description of it printed in the New York World:

The harbor probably has never witnessed a more picturesque scene than that of yesterday, when the Persian Monarch steamed up from Quarantine. Buffalo Bill stood on the captain's bridge, his tall and striking figure clearly outlined, and his long hair waving in the wind; the gaily painted and blanketed Indians leaned over the ship's rail; the flags of all nations fluttered from the masts and connecting cables. The cowboy band played "Yankee Doodle" with a vim and enthusiasm which faintly indicated the joy felt by everybody connected with the "Wild West" over the sight of home.

Shortly after my arrival I was much pleased by the receipt of the following letter:

## Fifth Avenue Hotel, New York. Colonel WM.F. Cody:

Dear Sir—In common with all your countrymen, I want to let you know that I am not only gratified but proud of your management and success. So far as I can make out, you have been modest, graceful, and dignified in all you have done to illustrate the history of civilization on this continent during the past century. I am especially pleased with the compliment paid you by the Prince of Wales, who rode with you in the Deadwood coach while it was attacked by Indians and rescued by cowboys. Such things did occur in our days, but they never will again.

As nearly as I can estimate, there were in 1865 about nine and one-half million of buffaloes on the Plains between the Missouri River and the Rocky Mountains; all are now gone, killed for their meat, their skins, and their bones. This seems like desecration, cruelty, and murder, yet they have been replaced by twice as many cattle. At that date there were about 165,000 Pawnees, Sioux, Cheyennes, and Arapahoes, who depended upon these buffaloes for their yearly food. They, too, have gone, but they have been replaced by twice or thrice as many white men and women, who have made the earth to blossom as the rose, and who can be counted, taxed, and governed by the laws of Nature and civilization. This change has been salutary, and will go on to the end. You have caught one epoch of this country's history, and have illustrated it in the very heart of the modern world—London—and I want you to feel that on this side of the water we appreciate it.

This drama must end; days, years, and centuries follow fast; even the drama of civilization must have an end. All I aim to accomplish on this sheet of paper is to assure you that I fully recognize your work. The presence of the Queen, the beautiful Princess of Wales, the Prince, and the British public are marks of favor which reflect back on America sparks of light which illuminate many a house and cabin in the land where once you guided me honestly and faithfully, in 1865-66, from Fort Riley to Kearney, in Kansas and Nebraska.

Sincerely your friend,

W.T. SHERMAN.

Our next descent on Europe was made in the steamer Persian Monarch, which was again chartered. This time our destination was France. The Parisians received the show with as much favor as had the Londoners.

Everything American became the fad during our stay. Fashionable young men bought American and Mexican saddles for their rides in the Bois.

Cowboy hats appeared everywhere on the street. There was a great cry for stories of the Plains and all the books that could be found that dealt with the West were translated into the French language. Relics from the Plains and mountains, bows, moccasins, and Indian baskets, sold like hot cakes in the souvenir stores.

While in the city I accepted an invitation from Rosa Bonheur to visit her at her superb château. In return I extended her the freedom of the show, and she made many studies from life of the fine animals I had brought over with me. She also painted a portrait of me on my favorite horse—a picture which I immediately sent home to my wife.

Our sojourn in Rome was lively with incident. The Prince of Simonetta, who visited the show, declared that he had some wild horses in his stable which no cowboy could ride. The challenge was promptly taken up by some of the dare-devils in my party. That the horses might not run amuck and injure anyone, special booths were erected in the show arena, where the trial was to be made.

The greatest enthusiasm was manifested by the Romans in the performance, and it was clear to me that most of them looked eagerly forward to the mortal injury of some of the members of my company. The Latin delight in sports like those of the old Roman arena had by no means died out.

When the horses were loosed in the ring they sprang into the air, snorted, kicked up their heels, and plainly defied any of the cowboys to do so much as to lay a hand on them. But in less time than I can tell it the plainsmen had sent their lassos hurtling through the air, and the horses discovered that they had met their masters. The audience, always strong for the winners, forgot their disappointment in the absence of fatalities, and howled with delight as the cowboys, one after another, mounted the fractious horses and trotted them submissively about the arena. We closed this tour of Europe, which was successful to the end, with a second visit to England.

I have now come to the end of my story. It is a story of "The Great West that Was," a West that is gone forever.

All my interests are still with the West—the modern West. I have a number of homes there, the one I love best being in the wonderful Big Horn Valley, which I hope one day to see one of the garden spots of the world.

In concluding, I want to express the hope that the dealings of this Government of ours with the Indians will always be just and fair. They were the inheritors of the land that we live in. They were not capable of developing it, or of really appreciating its possibilities, but they owned it when the White Man came, and the White Man took it away from them.

It was natural that they should resist. It was natural that they employed the only means of warfare known to them against those whom they regarded as usurpers. It was our business, as scouts, to be continually on the warpath against them when they committed depredations. But no scout ever hated the Indians in general.

There have been times when the Government policy toward the Indians has been unwise and unjust. That time, I trust, has passed forever. There are still many thousand Indians in the country, most of them engaged in agricultural pursuits. Indian blood has added a certain rugged strength to the characters of many of our Western citizens. At least two United States Senators are part Indian, and proud of it.

The Indian makes a good citizen, a good farmer, a good soldier. He is a real American, and all those of us who have come to share with him the great land that was his heritage should do their share toward seeing that he is dealt with justly and fairly, and that his rights and liberties are never infringed by the scheming politician or the short-sighted administration of law.

❒

9 789390 997664

Printed by Libri Plureos GmbH in Hamburg,
Germany